Dedication

To Edna, whose tales of tribulations
inspired us to see the pathos, humor, and
determination of our elders.

Patience is a virtue and a necessity.

Acknowledgments

W| e wish to thank the following people who answered specific queries, tracked down sources, and helped us clarify often confusing red tape and jargon.

Dave Armstrong, Episcopal Homes Foundation; Diane Morton, Hillsdale Manor Alzheimer's Center; Barbara Blusiewicz, Heatherwood Alzheimer's Care; Diane Driver, Center on Aging, Academic Geriatric Resource Program; University of California, Berkeley; Chris Alonzo, Stephanie Sanders-Badt, Philip Raiser, Danny Smith, Oliver Spencer, Karen Krebs, Ombudsman Inc., Carolyn Rosenbusch, Elizabeth Siegman, Judy Deibler, Eileen Bailey, Nancy Martin, Tom Shapiro, Donna Blondfield, Barbara Cullinane, Eva Meijer, Susan Carrington, Janet Meiselman, Suzanne McGuinn, Keri Clark, Bonnie Lawrence, Family Caregiver Alliance, Theresa Miller, Granger Cobb, Kathleen Adams, Patricia DeFrates, Paul Tunnell, Marcy Hara, Rosemary Koder, Charles Speers, Lee Taber, Chris Emerson, Rosemary O'Hara, Kimberly McCaughey, Vera Madison, Ann-Marie Meehan, Tim Alonzo, Ellen Seawall, and Peter Calfee. We are especially grateful to the hundreds of retirement community residents and their families who spoke candidly with us about their decision to move.

Table of Contents

Dedication iii

Acknowledgments iv

Introduction: *Parents* by Sally Quinn 1

Preface 12

1   Where Will My Parents Live? 19

2   Hard-to-Dodge Topics for Seniors 26

3   Should I or Shouldn't I Move? 39

4   If I Decide to Move, How Do I Choose
       the Right Place? 51

5   Housing Options for Seniors 58

6   Adapting the House to Meet
       the Seniors' Needs 69

7   Planned Adult Communities 81

8   Independent Retirement Communities 86

9   Rental Communities with Two, Three
       and Four Levels of Care. 95

10   Continuing Care and Lifecare Communities
       with No Equity 105

11   Continuing Care Communities with Equity. 114

12   Assisted Living Facilities 125

13   Choosing a Skilled Nursing Facility 129

14   Alzheimer's Facilities 139

15   Low Income and Subsidized Housing 147

16   Small Board and Cares 154

17   Sidestepping the Pitfalls of Moving 161

18   What To Know About Working With a Realtor
or Contractor When Selling or Remodeling
Your Parents' Home 179

19   Help! I Can Hardly Cope With My Own Life,
and Now My Parents Are Falling Apart! 192

20   "We Decided to Move When My Wife Closed
the Kitchen," and Other Gems From Seniors
and Their Children 217

Glossary 227
Comparative Cost Worksheet 236
Visitor's Checklist 237
Index 248
About the Authors 250

Parents

by Sally Quinn

I t seems that there are topics which dominate our lives at different junctures. We talk about our parents and schools and dates in our teens and early twenties. We talk about jobs and marriage and babies in our twenties and thirties and even early forties. But then something unexpected happens. We start talking about our parents again. This time it's how to take care of them. We aren't prepared for this. We are so used to having them take care of us, take care of our children, be our rock and our support. Suddenly, it changes. Suddenly, one of them gets sick and the other one is incapable of coping with the situation, so we step in. But it isn't as easy as it might seem. It is complicated. The sick parent doesn't want to admit physical frailty. The caretaking parent doesn't want to admit emotional frailty. The financial situation is unclear or unstable. Siblings have different opinions, are willing or able to take on varying degrees of responsibilities. Choices and options are numerous and difficult. Sides are taken, boundaries drawn. Grief and confusion and anger are overwhelming. Nobody knows what to do or where to go for help.

My sister Donna has written a wonderful book with Sarah Morse about exactly that. Not only is she an expert in the field and has had years experience dealing with this subject, she is a veteran herself of our own personal debilitating family crisis. I am thankful that I had Donna as my sister to guide us through the horrendous maze of doctors—neurologists, cardiologists and radiologists; care-givers, occupational and physical therapists, private nurses, real estate agents, bankers, accountants, movers, contractors, painters, geriatric psychiatrists, social workers, aging consultants, chiropractors, insurance agents, nutrition specialists, swimming therapists, and stroke clubs, to name just a few. We all made mistakes, but without Donna's help, surviving this most painful of experiences would have been unthinkable.

It seems that half my conversations with friends today are about taking care of their aging parents. I give them my sister's phone number. Most of them know my story. But for those who don't, let me tell you about our family and our experience. We are not unique.

"Bette," like Bette Davis, is the way she spells it. Lots of gals were named Bette in those days. It was a name for women who had bright smiles, sassy personalities and great legs. That was my mama. Sara Bette they called her in Statesboro, Georgia, but Savannah was more sophisticated and she became simply Bette. Mother was a brunette. Her older sister Maggie had blonde hair piled in curls on top of her head. They both looked fantastic in bathing suits and they tanned easily to a golden honey glow. They were by far the two most popular girls on the boardwalk and at the dances at Tybee Beach. They called themselves the "Hot-cha Sisters".

She was voted the "Best Legs in Savannah" and graced the float in the town parade as the Paper Queen. She rode horses and re-hearsed with the ballet Russe de Monte Carlo when they came through town, turning down their offer of a position at the insis-tence of her father. But Savannah was a small town and she wanted out. So when a handsome and gallant young lieutenant asked her to dance one night at the Officer's club at Port Screven, a nearby Army Post, she said "yes." And "yes" again to his proposal a week later. And "yes" at the altar a month later.

The world was a big place and Bette Quinn wanted to experience it all. Fort Benning, Georgia; Jacksonville, Florida, and small towns in Louisiana and Washington State were only the beginning. Then, after World War II when my father returned from Europe, it was Washington, D.C. and a whole new and sophisticated life of parties and people. From there it was three years in three cities in Japan during the Korean War, San Antonio, back to Washington, Alabama, Greece, Germany, Colorado, Washington State, back to Washington, D.C. and then off to Germany again to be the wife of the Commanding General of the Seventh Army.

"You are not in the army," my father had told her when they were married, "I am." She took that to heart, cutting a lovely swath through the various Army posts and town where we were stationed. Always independent, never kowtowing to anyone, just on the edge of iconoclasm, but never over the line, she danced, did she ever, to her own drummer.

Everyone loved her. She was beautiful and sexy and gay and graceful, and she loved nothing better than to have a good time. With her six-inch long cigarette holder, her Sortilege perfume and her glass of champagne, she charmed Generals and Admirals and Ambassadors, Chancellors, Emperors, Kings, Princes, Senators, Congressmen, and Presidents.

Her secret? She made everyone feel good about themselves, feel special. The life of the party, she gave life to everyone else. The shy person in the corner nobody would talk to? She would be there, drawing that person into the circle, welcoming them, including them. The famous person surrounded by everyone? That person would inevitably gravitate to where my mother was, telling stories, listening to stories, laughing and teasing and flirting. Having fun. The way to do that, she believed, was to make sure everyone else was having fun too. No malice, no envy, no jealousy, she was kind and generous to and about everyone. She gloried in the good fortune of others, their happiness was her happiness. Our happiness was her happiness. The people she loved, the people she cared about, could do no wrong. She was never too busy to listen, to talk, to commiserate, to praise, to bolster a bruised ego.

Her parties were the best. How could you not have a good time when your hostess was having such a ball? Her food was the greatest. She wrote a cookbook for her children. It was called "Plain Food for Fancy People". The kitchen was her kingdom. Good ole Southern fried cookin', combined with an eclectic assortment of foreign recipes she had collected from around the world. A big jar of bacon grease sat under the sink, just waiting to fry something, anything, in. Chicken and dumplin's, cornbread dressing, fried chicken, country ham, cheese grits, pork chops, and rice and gravy were just a few of her specialties.

"Ya'll want some more?" We would have been disappointed if she hadn't asked.

Just to hear her voice on the other end of the phone, "Hi, darlin'!" made one's heart leap up. Just to hear her exclaim at her own mischief, "Hot dog!" made one want to be with her. She was the heart of our family. She was where the joy was. She was a truly magical person.

On December the fifth, 1992, my mother had a stroke. She was home on that Sunday night, baby-sitting my 10 year-old son, Quinn, while my husband Ben and I were at the Kennedy Center Honors. She was in the kitchen, as usual, fixing Quinn his favorite dinner of hot dogs and baked beans while he watched television in her bedroom. My father was in the study reading. She adored baby-sitting for Quinn. He loved being with her as much as he liked being at home. He regularly spent two nights a week with my mother and father, nights which all three of them cherished. She cooked for him and gave him baths, served him breakfast in bed, rubbed his back at night and generally spoiled him to death. My father read Bible stories to him, started a coin collection with him and, with a set of metal Yankee and Rebel soldiers, played endless hours of Civil War with him.

My father is hard of hearing, so that when my mother collapsed on the kitchen floor, he didn't hear her moan. When Quinn came into the kitchen shortly afterwards, he screamed for my father to come and help, yet he still didn't hear. Quinn tried to help my mother up, but finding her unconscious, he ran terrified to my father, crying out to him to call 911.

When the ambulance came, they took Quinn with my mother and father in the back. Traumatized, he thought my mother was dead. Frantically, my father tried to reach Ben and me, without success. When we reached home a message was waiting and we rushed to the hospital. Ben took a shaken Quinn home while I stayed with my mother in intensive care.

She was paralyzed for a while and couldn't speak. Gradually through the night she began to get her speech back and, though weak, she began to move her arms and legs.

Finally, early the next morning, she fell asleep and I went home to get some sleep myself.

She had had heart problems for about ten years. Her doctors felt she was not a candidate for surgery, so she was being treated with medication. We had nagged and harangued and exhorted her so much she finally agreed to visit Pritikin the year before, but she didn't really like it and "fell off the wagon" soon after her return. She wasn't an exerciser and she really wasn't happy unless she had "grease running down her elbows" from her Southern cooking. She had had a couple of scares over the years, loss of feeling in her arms a few times, and throwing up and passing out once, all attributed to her condition, but nothing that really gave her "religion".

Because my father is in the Army, my parents have free medical care and are treated at Walter Reed Army hospital. However, the one thing the Army does not provide is long term care and my parents had no insurance for that. It was only much later that we would realize how important that would be. After my mother got out of the hospital her doctors put her on a regimen of medication and told her to rest.

On December 16th, they celebrated their 50th wedding anniversary with a buffet supper dance. Both of my parents are gregarious. My father is a tall, handsome, square-jawed Irishman, a great wit and raconteur, full of life and joy. My mother, genetically incapable of missing a party, sat at the entrance to the ballroom on a bar stool greeting guests. She danced one dance with my father at the end of the evening but it was a serious effort for her and she was visibly tired.

She wasn't able, for the first time in her life, to do her Christmas shopping that December. After opening presents, she couldn't stay for Christmas dinner. For the first time I had to do the turkey and gravy myself. The turkey was overcooked. The gravy was lumpy. New Year's Eve she stayed at home.

My son Quinn refused to go to her house, terrified that she might have another stroke. It broke her heart. But he was right. None of us could know that he would never spend another night with her again.

On the weekend of January the seventeenth, she suffered another stroke, this one down on the Eastern shore of Maryland in her country house. This time she was completely paralyzed, couldn't speak and she lost all cognitive ability. We had her taken by ambulance to Walter Reed where she stayed for over two months doing intensive therapy.

My brother and sister flew in from the West Coast, her friends rallied, we had a 75th birthday party for her on January the 27th. We did her hair, dressed her up, made her up, propped her up and wheeled her into a private room for birthday cake and champagne. She was unable to talk. It was painful and embarrassing, the more so because everyone was trying so hard to be upbeat and gallant. My father and I visited her every day taking turns. Everyone sent flowers and gifts, and eventually began to phone when she regained her ability to speak.

This was terribly difficult for my father, who is 10 years older than my mother, and was used to being taken care of himself. He was on his own and though he struggled valiantly we could see the toll it was taking on him. He ended up in the hospital himself, at one point, in a room down the hall, suffering from pneumonia.

Finally she was released, with a private nurse, to return home. That night, to celebrate, my father and I organized a catered dinner for 12 friends at home. With a new hairdo and new silk pajamas, and a great makeup job, she looked terrific. Everyone was ecstatic. She was on the road to recovery. Bolstered by new medications and an optimistic attitude we all looked forward to her resuming her old way of life.

Two weeks later she collapsed with another massive stroke. She has never recovered. At the hospital a week later we wheeled her into a small dining room for an Easter dinner which she couldn't eat. And we all knew that this was the beginning of a very stressful time. We could never have imagined how stressful.

For several months, my mother was paralyzed and could barely speak. When she recovered, her right arm and hand were permanently paralyzed, she could not get up and sit down without help. She could not chew her food or feed herself, she could not toilet herself, she could not walk without some assistance, and she had lost what the neurologists call "executive function." She was unable to initiate any plans or much conversation, though she could talk. She had excessive loss of memory. She would require full-time nursing care, seven days a week, 24 hours a day for the rest of her life.

Thank God for my sister Donna, the author of this book. She knew what to do, where to go for help and who to call. The situation was made more difficult by the fact that Donna lives in California and we live in Washington. We had so many decisions to make, so much to do.

Should she go to a nursing home? If so, which one? Should my father go? She said she would rather be dead. Donna found us a retirement community and it was decided they should live together with a full-time nurse to take care of my mother. They both resisted giving up their newly redecorated apartment, but it was too difficult for my father to handle. Meals became an enormous hurdle. He would sit up until one or two in the morning trying to plan menus to help the nurses, giving Mother a balanced, nutritious diet of pureed foods which he could also eat.

Everything she had done before fell to him. He was faced with countless decisions: where to find decent nurses, what kind of therapy she should have and how often, how to organize her friends' visits, what to do about her car.

We chose an apartment in a Marriott facility, and we had to sell the old apartment. That meant sorting through all of their things, without much help from my mother; deciding what to keep, how to dispose of things they couldn't keep, decorating, painting and designing the new apartment.

There were two major issues which made this terribly difficult for all of us. Finances were the biggest concern. My father had money, but without long-term insurance we were faced with a huge bite out of his retirement income, without knowing how much. The second, no less serious issue, was the loss of control for my father. A retired general, he had always been in command. Now, his life was falling apart and it was very difficult for him to deal with it. There were too many things he couldn't control. Tempers flared when little things went wrong. Everyone blamed everyone else. We all had different ideas about what should be done and how it should be done. In desperation I hired an "aging" consultant who was very disappointing and very expensive. The old apartment didn't sell for over a year, which caused a cash flow problem. There were several disasters with the nurses until we finally found a good agency.

Though they have a gorgeous penthouse apartment with a fabulous view, all their meals and maid service provided, my parents had a difficult adjustment to the Jefferson. It was partly because they were forced to make all new friends. But more than that, though it was only 10 minutes away from their old apartment, it was in Virginia, across the bridge, therefore geographically undesirable. And too, they realized that once they had "crossed that bridge," their lives would be irrevocably changed. They complained at first that it was "the land of the living dead," that their lives were not worth living. They were more in shock than depressed. My mother began talking about suicide and begging for us to hire Dr. Kervorkian to kill her. My father didn't believe in psychiatry and resisted any help. Finally, after a year, we found a good psychiatrist for my mother and got her on antidepressants.

Now 89 and 79, my parents have adjusted to the Jefferson, have made friends there, and are involved in many of the planned activities. They still have their country house where they go religiously every weekend, but there is no guarantee how long that will be possible. Their closest old friends have been wonderful and loyal, but they have less and less in common and they see each other less and less. It's hard, because my mother, unable to feed herself or swallow anything but pureed food, really can't eat out. Their once extensive social life is more or less over. For my father, the most difficult part of living at the Jefferson is walking past the library every day to go to the mailbox. They put out a red rose whenever someone in the building dies. Hardly a day goes by, he says, that he doesn't see a red rose.

It has been five years now since my mother had her first stroke. During that period all of our lives, not just my parents lives but the lives of my brother and sister, my sister's children, my son and my husband have been drastically changed. The events of the past two years, physical, emotional and financial have been traumatic and devastating to the whole family. Our happiness, our lives and our relationships have been irrevocably shattered.

I have a photograph on my desk of my family taken on Thanksgiving Day, ten days before my mother's first stroke. It's a joyous picture. We are all smiling at the camera, arms around each other.

I remember my father saying prophetically to me that night, as we were heading off to bed, "I've never felt such love and such warmth as I have today. It will never be like this again."

Preface

In our research, we have seen many people who take charge of their lives. They have planned how, where, and with whom they will live in their older years. These Seniors are relatively healthy, productive people, able to function independently, and who have prepared for their future. On the other hand, Seniors who avoid facing the inevitable aging process, and think they will just die conveniently in their sleep, are often the most traumatized by a sudden move. This move is usually precipitated by a crisis. As seventy-one year-old Hilde put it, "There was so much confusement going on, I just signed the paper without reading it." How much better to plan for one's eventual old age, rather than being hostage to it. Most people who are financially secure look forward to their retirement years. For the majority, with careful planning and sound advice, options are available for comfortable alternative living situations. However, economic conditions limit choices for many. But, all is not lost. Even Seniors on low fixed incomes can find viable housing options in this country. Many will be living with families, but is that practical in cases where the Senior's health deteriorates to the point where they require constant supervision and care? Lastly and most commonly, a large segment of the Senior population will remain in their own homes. While staying in the old familiar home is feasible in many cases, new problems surface that will need to be addressed. Our clients' questions have included: "How much will it cost to adapt my house to meet my physical limitations?", "Since they discontinued the bus, there's no public transportation, so how is a companion going to get here?", "Where can we find a qualified caregiver?", "What'll we do about Dad neglecting the condition of his house?", "Should my parents stay in their home when their old friends have died or moved away and they don't know any of the new neighbors?" As difficult as it is to wrestle with all the issues and the basic desire to remain in comfortable surroundings, we encourage families to explore all the options before making a decision.

Directing our research and efforts to those who feel they are ready to explore a change, we have given reasons to encourage them to think congregate living can be viable and positive. Included are specifics on how to implement this change.

Five years ago, a lawyer called to say his client, Zelma Herman, a wealthy woman with no children, had suffered a stroke. He asked if I knew where she could live—a place with the same ambiance as her palatial estate. Wanting to help, I replied "yes," then realized I didn't know the first thing about what my grandmother called

"God's waiting room." Two hundred miles, eight low-sodium salad bars, and twenty-seven hours later, I discovered there were some very appealing communities. I found a fabulous place, sorted her belongings, organized the estate sale, oversaw the move, and made her new apartment a home. This is how my business, Ultimate Moves, a one-stop shop for Seniors and their families, was born. I visited over two hundred retirement communities during a six-month period, re-writing and evaluating my checklist.

Thank God I had some knowledge about the process of children needing to make decisions for their parents. Little did I know, two years after my mother's stroke, I'd be facing this crisis with my own parents. It didn't make it any easier that I had Ultimate Moves because the emotional impact on your life is something you can't be prepared for. At this point, Sarah Morse, a writer friend who was searching for a suitable place for her 88 year-old aunt, joined the business. Sarah pointed out that our friends' conversations had run the gamut from our pregnancies, recalcitrant teenagers, their SAT scores, graduate schools and jobs, to our current common concern which was, you guessed it, the dilemma of why, when, and how to take charge of our parents' future. After Ultimate Moves was launched and my name became recognized by people in the field, I was approached by groups to give talks on the differences in retirement communities and how to make the move easier. I didn't set out to be a consumer advocate, but as I saw how the elderly are taken advantage of, it seemed an injustice to not mention precautions older people should take to protect themselves. I kept hearing, "You have all this information, why don't you put it in a book because just about everybody is going through it?" So we did it.

We outlined our plan. Considering how many different options were in the Bay Area, we targeted a random sampling from our data base, and added new communities to visit. A hundred seemed the magic number. Of course, we planned our arrival to coincide with lunch at the most appealing dining rooms. And as for humor, there was no shortage. How can you keep a straight face when Josie, an animated 79 year-old, remarked, "If I start to die from the head first, shoot me." On the same day, we overheard Elizabeth talking to a friend, "I just asked how you were, I certainly didn't expect an organ recital." And how we roared when the administrator of one of the most state-of-the-art Alzheimer's facilities forgot our appointment. As soon as we visited a place, one would scribble the observations and complete the forms while the other overshot the freeway exit for the tenth time. Several directors wanted our questionnaires, many were defensive and suspicious, but most remarked that this project was definitely timely and needed. The response from older people to our undertaking was echoed by 93 year-old JoEllen, "If only we'd had this book when we were looking for a place to live, we wouldn't have chosen a place where I have to carry Blinky, my Chihuahua, from my apartment to the sandbox so she wouldn't wee-wee in the elevator."

Once the idea went past go, we defined the most typical levels of retirement living, realizing we should see a broad spectrum catering to all socio-economic groups. Since we had both sought help for our parents, devising a checklist with provocative questions seemed easy; we thought we'd covered just about everything. But, as we toured facilities, listening to administrators, marketing directors, and especially the residents, we became aware of issues so crucial to

making a good decision that we revised, added, and deleted questions. It took a lot more time than we anticipated. We then conducted focus groups to hear what Seniors and their children had to say. One group was for people who had moved to a retirement community, a second was held in the Senior centers for participants to explain their reasons for moving or staying put, and more focus groups were for children of aging parents.

The Seniors were in their element in these sessions. Feelings emerged as they let down their guard, laughing and relating funny and poignant stories from their past. They invited us to their rooms to show us their treasures, and they cried recalling their salad days. We got the bright idea to snare them into the focus groups where we held drawings with certificates to the Sizzler salad bar (they were gladly donated), which they loved and fought over.

We haunted libraries, begged anyone who had statistics to share, met with gerontologists, bugged American Association of Retired Persons (AARP) for their information, while balancing clients, move-in jobs, and travel to the East and Southeast for relocations. Finally, it was time to summarize, condense, sort out, and get down to the task of creating a helpful, informative book.

The sandwich generation is "in" these days, and everybody is talking and writing about our parents—how to help them, where they should go, why they should or shouldn't stay in their houses, how to keep them solvent while we retain our sanity, and what to do when a parent needs care. How is our book different? We didn't stop at merely explaining the different types of retirement communities, we've gone one step further by addressing the anxiety and the overwhelming fear that many Seniors confront at a major change in their lifestyle. "How do I get myself organized for a move?" prompted us to develop guidelines that will help them start the process. We've pinpointed in one book many of the issues that parents and children will face when they deal with the overwhelming thought of moving. Retirees will find a community they like, but it often takes them two or three years to make the move because the thought of actually moving is so traumatizing. They think the option will always be there, but it's a sad sight when the Admissions Director has to tell them they can't move in because their health has declined.

Our book focuses on what we saw, which in many cases is different from what the brochure depicts and what the marketing director is selling. We've compiled significant insightful data. We tell you what isn't in the contract, and alert you as to what you're most likely to encounter, and we've included case studies and anecdotes to illustrate our points. We give you facts, tell you what to ask, and warn you of possible pitfalls. You'll learn the real scoop on buy-ins with equity, and we'll point out under what circumstances you or your estate would receive a refund if you move to a continuing care community and later decide to leave. We'll let you know that sometimes the marketing staff will refrain from telling you the name of the skilled nursing facility they have a contract with because so many people know the nursing home's reputation. And there's a chapter for people with low and middle incomes. Some of this may be familiar to you, but a lot of it may not. We have had the opportunity to talk with people who have been through all of this before, or are presently going through it, and we have compiled it all here. You are certain to learn from their experience, including what they did right, as well as what they would do differently.

1.
Where Will My Parents Live?

O kay, you've raised your children, fretted about your health, and wondered if you'd still have a job tomorrow—what's next on the list to give you gray hair? If you guessed coping with aging parents, go to the head of the class. What is your bigger concern—your parents' living or your parents' dying? Either one is likely to wreak havoc in your mid-life. And you are not alone. At least one in four Americans struggles with this issue. The reality is that some people's older years are so miserable they and their families hope they can just check out peacefully. It's not that we wish for their death, it's that we want our parents to live their later years enjoying the best quality of life possible. Most of us are guilt-ridden entertaining such thoughts, and we wonder where to go to surrender. While many factors are beyond one's control, there are steps to take that could make a difference.

Roughly 22% of our country's work force is expected to face concerns relating to aging parents, and one of the major issues confronting families is where will my parents live? As we were researching this book, we realized just how difficult it is for Seniors and their children to gather information, especially without any knowledge or background in the field. Trying to get relevant information on housing and other Senior issues is an exercise in frustration. When we tried to reach Senior agencies, we were transferred around the country, put on hold for inordinate amounts of time,

couldn't understand the receptionist's English, and were cut off more times than our kid's jeans! We encountered administrators and supervisors in many facilities who didn't understand some of the subtleties and variations in their own types of communities, let alone many of the others. Now put yourself in the shoes of your frail, hard-of-hearing mother who doesn't always remember if she fed the cat. Do you think she could gather information, understand it, orchestrate it, and make a move on her own? Hardly! And, after working hard all week, do children want to spend their evenings and weekends gathering pamphlets, scrutinizing contracts, and visiting places to come up with an appropriate spot that will take Mom and Dad? And don't think it will be a piece of cake convincing your brothers and sisters that you picked a winner.

Many families share the same concerns. They feel helpless in their inability to cope with the magnitude of a move, and sadness at their parents leaving the family home. On the other hand, the kids know that Mom and Dad can't make it any longer on their own. What to do? We saw how this turmoil could create disagreements and tension. They expressed fear of the unknown and insecurity as to whether they could handle all the details to insure a smooth transition. Children become frightened when they witness a parent's frailty and deterioration. The parents want to control their own lives, while the children wrestle with what they feel would be best for their mother and father. This role reversal is unsettling for everyone, even though parents are often relieved to have the decisions taken from their hands.

The scenarios vary: perhaps Dad suffered a stroke and Mom was unable to care for him, or Mom was forgetful and the daughter felt she couldn't remain in her own home. The bottom line was always the same—"How can we find out about available housing choices, what they will cost, and what kind of shape must I be in to get my foot in the door?" And if that is not enough, "How on earth are we going to accomplish it all and remain sane?"

A good retirement community offers an attractive alternative to living alone in your own home. Beyond being offered independence, security, and a variety of stimulating activities, people have a chance to enjoy a sense of community and to make new, lasting friendships. It is very important to weigh all of the pros and cons of moving against remaining in your own home, as this could be the most important move of your life. Whatever your choice of living situation, you'll need to face the inevitable decline of your health or your parents' health. We can't stress enough the need to be prepared for a crisis that may well occur. It is far more difficult for the family to cope in time of an emergency when there is no contingency plan. Start by formulating a plan to explore your and your parents' options, and to understand them while they are in good health. If you follow our suggestions, you will be in far better shape emotionally and financially. According to AARP, "residents of all income levels who fail to plan adequately ahead and or move too quickly, are more likely to choose inappropriate housing that doesn't meet their needs and preferred lifestyle."

As we age, the following questions warrant consideration: How much control should children assume when dealing with their aging parents?, Should children take the lead and initiate their parents' move, or should parents be expected to be responsible for their living situations?, How does one know when to step in and offer a hand or advice?, Why don't our parents reach out for help?, When is the right time to begin the search for the best place?, and Is it imperative that every Senior eventually move from his/her home? A recent AARP survey revealed that nearly 70% of older Americans would consider some form of supportive living. The same survey indicates that 54% have done nothing or very little regarding the planning of their housing needs for later years.

After seeing the positive changes take place in the lives of the older adults we have moved to retirement communities, we must disagree with those who advocate Seniors staying in their own homes as long as they can. While this may seem ideal, it has the potential to create a negative situation for many. The longer one waits, the fewer choices are available. When we conducted focus groups with healthy Seniors living in congregate living situations, we found the number-one issue affecting the decision to move was "loneliness and isolation." Singles seem to benefit greatly by making a move, whereas some couples feel they don't have to consider it as they have each other. Couples move for a variety of reasons: to gain independence from home maintenance, because one spouse may be suffering from failing health, or to be able to travel anxiety-free. Should a spouse die, the transition from marriage to being alone is eased by the comfort and support of friends in their community. Take Mr. and Mrs. Lamby, who had lived in their home for 52 years. After falling and injuring her hip, Mrs. Lamby's mobility was so impaired that staying home didn't make sense, as her husband was having a hard time caring for her. Neither wanted a stranger in the house. They decided to move to a Lifecare community close to their home. Six months later, Mrs. Lamby died. As the widowed Mr. Lamby told us, it was a blessing living in a place where he could rely on his friends for comfort, and where he didn't have to go through the process of sorting and moving from his home alone.

This book is for those who may be intimidated by bureaucracy and by parents who refuse to acknowledge their predicament. For those of us forced to parent our parents, the emotional cost is high. We must re-define the relationship, guide our parents to acceptance of the new roles, try to understand it ourselves, and realize our anger and fear is often based on past family history. It is uncomfortable and not easy to master. Our client Wendy told us the hardest part of mothering her mother was being the guardian of her dignity.

Our questions, answers, and insights will help families avoid the hurdles they may encounter in choosing appropriate housing, and ease the transition of moving their parents from a home to a congregate living community. The following questions are typical of what we've been asked. Do you recognize any?

1. "My elderly husband's a menace on the road after two drinks, tranquilizers, glaucoma and a heart condition. What can I do?"

2. "Does Ensure do what it implies, since that and one martini is Mom's dinner?"

3. "Do anti-depressants help when your parents constantly talk about suicide?"

4. "Is there a shortcut to figuring out the Medicare bills?"

5. "How do I tell my aging parents I don't want them to live with me?"

6. "Is there a kind way to let my mother know I don't want her to care for my children any more?"

7. "Should I embarrass my parents by offering to pay their cleaning bills so they don't wear dirty clothes?"

8. "What should I do when my uncle's nursing home requests that I give a 'contribution?'"

9. "My wife leaves not one, but several lighted cigarettes burning around the house, and it terrifies me—what can I do?"

10. "Our 89 year-old father wants to marry his 33 year-old nurse; do you think it's a good idea?"

2.

Hard-to-Dodge Topics For Seniors

W|e can't possibly cover all the issues confronting families with aging parents, as health, economic situations, and family dynamics will affect each case differently. However, you'll recognize many of the following:

"My parents need to make some decisions about their lives, but are unwilling to face the problems."

First of all, are they capable of making sound decisions? If not you may need some professional help in assessing their situation.

There are several red flags in determining the ability of your parents to make life decisions, generally accepted in the legal world, and here they are:

■ Can the person make and express any choices concerning his/her life?

■ Are the outcomes of these choices reasonable?

■ Are these choices based on rational reasons?

■ Is the person able to understand the personal implications of the choices that are made?

■ Does the person actually understand the implications of those choices?

If you've determined that your parents are capable of being in charge, don't get your hopes up that they'll follow your advice. If they're unwilling to listen to you, try sending them a letter spelling out some of the issues worth addressing and let them know the consequences if they don't. For instance, an expired driver's license results in canceled insurance in many states. A couple of good magazine articles can work wonders, as consequence stories deliver the message. Pride, ego and trust are major players here, because the issues are losing control and giving in, part of the old parent/child conflict. Parents have to think they are part of the process, but at the same time, they need to trust their children's instincts.

"I feel tremendous frustration seeing my parents fall apart. I want to help them, but I don't know where to start, and how much I should do."

Take action. Try open communication about their situation, and let them know they're not alone. Don't wait until a crisis hits; begin discussing alternatives while they can be part of the solution. Now is a good time to take advantage of volunteers, to learn what's available in your parents' community. Contact nursing organizations, religious groups, service clubs, and city and county educational and outreach programs. You can consult senior organizations, physician referral services, advertisements in senior periodicals, and

elder care groups. Be sure to take care of yourself by being organized and recognizing that your needs are important—you can't
baby your parents. You would be a real exception if you didn't feel
overwhelmed. The stress and sadness of watching a loved one's
decline can drain the hardiest soul. One woman told us it was like
being caught in the eye of a hurricane. And don't buy into the guilts,
you can't assume the responsibility for making a parent happy. Sue,
a client, developed an ulcer realizing she was becoming too en-
meshed in her parents lives. This can be a trap of which we must all
beware.

Children assuming responsibility for their aging parents.

Often it's not only advisable, but necessary for everybody's
well-being to assume the responsibility for parents' decisions. Use
your intuition here; if you feel there's the potential for life threaten-
ing consequences, don't be shy. Sarah and Betty's mother suffered a
stroke. Her physician recommended a standard medication in treat-
ing stroke patients. Dad hadn't paid attention to the doctor's advice
and refused to listen to his daughters when they pleaded with him
to be sure she was taking the proper medicine. He assured them he
was in control when, in fact, she wasn't taking the medicine at all.
Four days after being discharged, she suffered a massive stroke. The
daughters, of course, blamed themselves for not taking charge, when
they knew Dad might be inattentive.

Paying for our parents' old age.

There's more than one way to skin a cat, and here they are:

parents paying for themselves, family members (this can mean you kids) chipping in, good old Uncle Sam, or the prudent person who buys long term care insurance. Of course, there are exceptions to everything; maybe Ed MacMahon will be at your mother's door with the big check. For those planning to foot the bill themselves, a good financial advisor or estate planner who specializes in retirement and who understands the potential cost of medical care is the best way. But don't consult just anyone from the yellow pages—ask for a referral from your local Bar Association, or a Certified Financial Planner in good standing with the International Board of Standards and Practices for Certified Financial Planners, Inc. The National Academy of Elder Law Attorneys offers information on selecting an estate planner or elder law attorney.

Connie and her two brothers had to financially help Zenna,

who was in her eighties, so she could live in the type of retirement community she preferred. They each chipped in a couple hundred dollars monthly. When brother Jeff was on the shorts, the others carried him until he was able to cover his share. Wouldn't it be great if this was the happy scenario in every family? Medicaid, funded by the states and the federal government, provides medical care, with eligibility based on financial status. The government may pay for your parents if they need assistance with daily living, but you should check on the financial issues regarding eligibility in the state where they plan to spend their last years. As for a nursing home, each state decides eligible groups, types, and ranges for services, payment levels and procedures within broad federal guidelines.

Another option is long term care insurance coverage, which has seen tremendous growth over the last five years. Today, about 10% of those over 65 are covered by this type of coverage. This covers an individual when he/she experiences a chronic illness, such as Parkinson's disease, hypertension, arthritis, Alzheimers, etc., or an injury that does not necessarily require continuous hospitalization. Often, it's defined as nursing home care, but it's important to realize that long term care is frequently provided in the home. These services can also include household chores or personal care services not provided by health care professional.

Supplemental insurance covering nursing home costs.

Supplemental insurance covers only the difference in what Medicare pays and what you owe. Suzanne, 70, and her 92 year-old mother, Glenda, had lived together for 22 years. Suzanne had been in charge of her mother's affairs and had purchased a supplemental insurance policy from AARP, assuming that Mom's medical needs would be covered. Suzanne was feeling as if she had the world on a string. Then the inevitable happened. Glenda had a stroke and wound up in a skilled nursing facility. When asked what kind of insurance she carried to cover the cost of the nursing home, Suzanne replied, AARP's supplemental insurance. Much to her chagrin, the administrator told her she was out of luck. This was a devastating blow to both women, because four years later, with her mother still in the nursing home, Suzanne was destitute and living with a cousin. The bottom line is: know what you're buying, know what it covers and especially, know what it *doesn't* cover.

Dealing with parents who live in another city.

You live across the country from Mom and get the dreaded phone call telling you there's a crisis. You'll probably have to go to the scene. Plan to look at the whole picture to assess the situation, being as realistic as possible. If you can't physically stay in Mom's area, find a good case manager who is capable of handling all the problems—from nuts to bolts. Someone else has to be the child and do the research, and implement the changes. You'll have to trust the person and make sure your parent, too, is comfortable with him/her. Start by calling Eldercare Locator, an information hot line that can direct you to services in your parents' area. And don't forget to check references thoroughly. Also, you'll need to devise a plan for the worst case scenario. Get names and references while you're there in case your parent has to check into a facility offering more medical services. It's important to reassure your parent that this person you retain will be there for moral support, advice and physical help. This might be the time to consider having your parents move near you. Weigh all the pros and cons of such a move and ask yourself: how much is it going to cost me to visit?, what if Dad has to go into a nursing home—how often will I get there?, and will they be more secure knowing I'm closer? Be prepared to make a commitment to seeing this problem through, even if that means more trips and more phoning. It's difficult to run a life from across the country.

Be concerned about a non-family member with ulterior motives becoming more important than you to an aging relative.

Older people can develop strong ties to their caregivers and often defend them to the hilt—after all, this person is with them most of the time. We've seen cases where older people become emotionally and physically dependent on their caregivers. If you're not around much, and not paying attention, chances are you may have to face the unpleasant task of terminating someone who has gained too much control. Don't feel intimidated to ask questions of anyone new in your parents' lives, and establish a relationship with all their care providers so you can count on them to contact you if they have concerns.

Uncle Harold's nurse seemed the perfect solution until the family realized that nobody was seeing him. After comparing notes, it turned out Miss Fisher was keeping him away from his relatives. Next thing the family knew, she'd married him, and when he died, they learned she'd inherited six million dollars. After lengthy litigation and a lot of mudslinging, the family was still out all the millions. In retrospect, they had only themselves to blame—they were so thrilled to be relieved of the burden of Harold's care, it didn't dawn on them to be suspicious. Above all, have a contract with any caregiver that includes a probationary period and regularly scheduled reviews, and make it understood that final decisions are your responsibility, and your orders are not to be rescinded or overridden. If you are in the vicinity, plan to drop in unannounced at least bi-monthly. Schedule regular doctor appointments so you know, as well as the caregiver, what's going on medically and what condition your elderly relative is in.

Understanding the difference between Lifecare and Continuing Care.

Continuing Care promises to provide one or more elements of care for the duration of a resident's life in exchange for payment of an entrance fee and periodic charges. Lifecare (a continuing care contract) promises to provide *all* levels of care, including acute care and physicians' services for the duration of life. The care is provided in a facility with a continuum of care, including a skilled nursing facility under the ownership and supervision of the provider on or adjacent to the premises. No change is made in the monthly fee based on the level of service. Most of the Lifecare and Continuing Care communities with whom we've been associated contain a provision to subsidize residents who become unable to pay their monthly care. We tell our clients, in Continuing Care you'll pay more at each level as you need additional assisted living, skilled nursing, etc. In Lifecare, you won't pay any extra as you need additional medical services.

Huntington and Muffy Chatfield moved into a Continuing Care Retirement Community because the entrance fee was less than the Lifecare Community down the street. The fact that Continuing Care was "pay as you go" appealed to them. After her dressage lesson three months after moving in, Muffy had a heart attack, and woke up in the skilled nursing unit of their retirement complex. Sure enough, two weeks later they received the first of many bills requiring them to pay for charges in the nursing wing. Had they moved into a Lifecare Community paying more initially, they'd be home free, paying no additional cost for her care.

"I've heard that after 2½ years in a nursing home most people have used up their resources—this really scares me and I'm wondering if it's true."

Yes, it's a fact in California and in many other states. The average cost for a year in a nursing home is $40,000 ($45,000 in California) and the cost is expected to rise by an estimated 7% annually, according to the U.S. Congressional Study on Aging, and the average stay is two and a half years. With the median net worth of households headed by retirees being $73,472, having to spend two years in a nursing home could result in poverty if they fail to plan ahead for this possibility.

Determining the best place for our parents.

Right off the bat, line up a physical, financial, emotional and needs assessment. Start with a doctor. What mental and physical shape is your father (or mother) in now, and what is the prognosis for his condition as he ages? Next, figure out what he (she) can afford, factoring in inflation increases. As for an emotional assessment, it's very important to try to understand what your parents are going through in leaving their current home and making what very well may be their final move. The next logical step involves making a needs assessment, and it is a lucky family that can compile this list together. The needs assessment should include:

■ Lifestyle—Urban vs. country, or does Dad like to putter outside?

■ Religious affiliation—Is this important?

■ Outside interests—Do your parents have hobbies or recreational activities that are accessible? If Mom is passionate about golf, is a course nearby?

■ Climate—Would Uncle Thad like Las Vegas in July?

■ Services, amenities—How close is the deli?

■ Contract and ownership provisions—Can you sell the apartment yourself, must you use their sales agents, and can you rent it?

■ Project history—Has the place been around a long time?

■ Background and socio-economic makeup of residents—
Who said our parents aren't picky?

■ General atmosphere—Does it seem like a good fit?

■ Physical condition and layout—Will Dad have to hike on
the ice to get to the dining room?

■ Good public transportation—How's Aunt Charlotte going
to get to her string quartet practice?

■ Attitude and responsibility of management and employees—Are they constantly passing the buck?

■ Quality of care—Do residents appear well-groomed and
cared for? Is Grandpa strolling the grounds unshaven in a
bathrobe?

■ Residents rights—Is this list available?

■ Quality of meals—Is everything fried and greasy?

■ Activities—Are they varied and appealing to your Mother?

■ Location—Do you want to be near Dad?

Beaulah loved her apartment at Sunny Farms, a pleasant Independent Retirement Community, and when she had to go to a
nursing facility after breaking her hip, her family didn't worry—
she'd be home soon. But while she was a patient a few miles away,
Sunny Farms declared bankruptcy, and all the residents had to be
out within 45 days. Her kids, more frustrated than ever, had to start

the search from scratch while Mom could only apologize for being a burden.

"I'm worried about what's going to happen to me when I need help because I have no friends or relatives."

If you're worrying now then you obviously understand the severity of the situation. Make a plan now. Assess your financial affairs by sitting down with a trusted estate planner who will do some research and be able to advise you. Perhaps it's not too late to consider long term care insurance and remember, the longer one waits to purchase insurance, the more it will cost. Learn what's available in living choices, and get out and visit several places. This is a time to trust other's advice—either a clergyman, lawyer, your physician or an acquaintance. We've seen so many older people in unpleasant situations that could've been avoided had they taken control of their lives when they were energetic and able. If you're in this predicament, you have to begin by helping yourself.

"I'm wondering if my father's short-term memory loss is Alzheimer's disease or some other form of dementia."

Dementia, the loss of such intellectual functions as thinking, remembering, and reasoning to the extent that daily functioning is impaired, is caused by more than 70 disorders. Alzheimer's disease is a specific neurological illness which usually begins with memory loss, disorientation and confusion, and as it progresses, there's further memory loss, as well as loss of reasoning and ability to care for one's self. The first step is to seek an accurate diagnosis by a competent medical professional, and you can get a referral by calling the Alzheimer's Association at 800-272-3900.

3.
Should I or Shouldn't I Move?

T he decision to move at any time in our lives is a major event, but as we advance in age it becomes even more difficult to make changes. We have advocated making the choice to move yourself, when you are healthy and have taken the time to research the best possible living situation. When planned this way, it provides a sense of control you may not otherwise have, and makes the transition a much easier one. If the choice is taken away from you, for whatever reasons, the move is much more traumatic for you and your family. Even if you have health problems, you may still be able to choose a living arrangement, if not in your home, which would be agreeable to you. Citing a study done by the Stanford Research Institute, we see four psychological factors that affect moving decisions.

■ *Social activity.* This is the level to which Seniors wish to have social involvement—extroverted versus introverted.

■ *Self indulgence,* or how much people are looking for gratification.

■ *Resistance to change.* Are they adaptable and flexible, and willing to absorb some change in their lives?

■ *Independence.* Do people want to be on their own, or are they seeking a stable network of support?

This chapter is broken up into five categories. One thing to keep in mind is that you may spend as many as 15 years in your new home, so weigh each issue carefully.

Financial Issues

The cost of living in your own home versus living elsewhere is the major consideration, especially if you are on a fixed income. Everything from the sewer tax to cleaning out the gutters needs to be addressed. How much available cash do you have on hand? If you move to a community, will you have enough money to pay for the yearly increases in your monthly assessment which every community has? Do you have enough money for the move? If you sell your house, are you aware of the closing costs you are responsible for in escrow? What are the tax implications of selling your home? Some people ask if they should move from their large single family home to a smaller one? Depending on where you move, this could have considerable impact on your property taxes, on a new loan cost if you do not pay cash, and on the capital gains tax you would have to pay.

Depending on your age and health, moving to a condo, for instance, where the maintenance is done by someone else can be a good approach. If you are older and are experiencing some health problems, we do not recommend a move in that direction. It doesn't seem to make much sense to move twice. If you are thinking of downsizing and are not in particularly good health, then make just one move to a community that has some medical assistance. How much did your house cost and how much has it appreciated? Are you going to rent or buy? Reverse mortgages, which allow you to take a lump sum or monthly payments against the equity in your house, can help you stay in your home if you are house poor. There are many restrictions and qualifications on these, so if you decide on this course of action, make sure you understand this option well before jumping in feet first. A charitable remainder trust is one way to approach the capital gains problems that plague many Seniors, especially if you are moving to a non-profit continuing care community. If you have a mortgage on your home, do you need that write-off to offset an income or is your home paid off? If you sell your home, and do not have a large income, will you have enough money from the sale to live comfortably in another community for the rest of your life?

Let's talk about the possibility of becoming ill and needing in-home care. Do you have enough money to stay in your home and have someone come in and care for you on a 24 hour basis, knowing this can cost as much as $4,000 per month. If not, do you have long term care insurance that will cover a portion of this care? Most communities have different levels of care and there is a cap on the amount it will cost, proportionate to the level of care provided. Another consideration is the cost of maintenance to the house. Is your home in good condition or have you neglected normal repairs over the years? This is an important issue if you are thinking of selling. If so, you will need to spend money at some point on maintenance. Last, but not least, is your house suitable for an older person who has become frail? Would you have enough money to remodel your home to your future physical limitations knowing that this could cost big bucks? This concern might not seem important now, but it is a factor in determining whether you can stay in your home.

Use a worksheet to compare the monthly costs of living at home versus the monthly costs of living in a community. It is extremely important to weigh all the factors involved, and not fall into the trap of deciding one or two of the issues do not apply to you. My mother was dancing and having a wonderful time and the next thing we knew, she was paralyzed. It can happen to all of us, so take the blinders off and realistically assess your situation. It may be time to hire a financial advisor or estate planner who specializes in working with Seniors.

Psychological Issues

One of the ladies in our focus groups told us adamantly that no one can understand the feelings older people face as they age unless he or she is a senior. We can only surmise. The reality of growing older is one thing, the fear is another. We all know that aging is inevitable, but how we as individuals choose to deal with it is another thing. Let's look at the fears that sometimes paralyze us and keep us from making important decisions about our future. As Carolee told us, the resistance Seniors show is really an expression of their fear and their hope that no one knows they are afraid.

The six most common concerns we heard about moving versus staying were:

1. "If I stay in my home I will be a burden to my children, and I promised myself that would never happen."

2. "If I move I will lose control over my life and my independence."
3. "I can't stand the thought of moving from my family home with all the memories."
4. "Even though I have friends, I often feel lonely and isolated living here alone."
5. "The security of congregate living really appeals to me."
6. "All my neighborhood friends have either died or moved away."

Senior's fears of growing older are based on their perception of what they will be like when they are old, and because they don't know what to expect, they don't know if they will be able to care for themselves. Many felt if they moved they would be dependent, restricted, and in some ways were "giving up." The fear of change and of the unknown were big reasons for people to stay in their homes, even when they knew it was not the best decision. And they expressed fear of being confined to a much smaller space.

If Seniors stay in their own homes, the responsibility of making decisions will likely fall on the shoulders of the children, as the parents slowly become unable to care for themselves. Moving can alleviate the problem, as a community can offer assistance in ways the children can't. A frequent remark was, "I never realized what freedom I would have if I moved out of my house." Living in a retirement community does not mean you lose control of your freedom, it's actually the reverse. Granted, giving up something you love, such as a home, is a very sad and traumatic event for many, but looking at the positive side can help the transition. A pertinent question to ask might be, "Why live in a house where you are all alone with no one to talk to, eating alone (if at all), and watching TV all day?" So, if you fear growing older and not being able to care for yourself, or you are alone, then moving may be the perfect solution, and the wisest choice for your future. The psychological well-being of our parents is a primary concern. Many people experience a rebirth when they move.

Health Issues

The ability to care for oneself in an acceptable way is a major concern for Seniors living alone. As they age, their increased physical limitations, and the worry they experience about how they will care for themselves without disrupting the lives of their children, keeps them in a state of anxiety most of the time. As we know, this stress can do nothing but exacerbate the problem. Insecurity and old patterns can lead to a less active lifestyle. When Jonathan went to see his parents, after not seeing them for a year, he was overwhelmed at the deterioration he saw in their living condition and was even more alarmed to realize his parents didn't even see the change. Things kept getting worse and they just adapted. He said he had to throw away some clothes because the cleaners said they were too far gone to be cleaned. And to think they may have been going out looking like that.

Other than personal hygiene, the lack of proper nutrition is a serious problem. Norma fought her kids about moving, saying she was doing just fine. When the kids came to visit from another state, they were appalled to discover nothing but Ensure cans, candy wrappers, and coffee cans in her garbage. She had lost 40 pounds

and looked like a skeleton. The deteriorating situation of aging in place is a difficult one to handle. Fear of accidents that could force Seniors to move weigh on them. If Mom and Dad are living alone without family nearby, ask yourself what happens if they become incapacitated and can't get help for a long period of time? And consider the partner who can no longer take care of his or her failing spouse. Many go from doctor to doctor getting different medications, sometimes taking the wrong amounts and often mixing medications that can be harmful to them. Even though many Seniors wear Life Line systems around their necks to alert the paramedics, you still need to remember to put it around your neck. So, it might be time to consider a move. If your parents can still drive, they can at least get out in the world and do things for themselves. If not, they are really captives in their own home.

Personal Issues

Loss of a spouse is often a catalyst for making the decision to move, although it may be better to wait awhile to avoid making decisions in haste, which could just create more problems. The majority of the moves in which we have assisted were for men and women who had recently lost a mate. Consider Gladys, whose husband's death was followed within two months by the deaths of her neighbors on either side. She felt totally isolated. She didn't drive, her son lived in another part of the state, and she had to rely on her neighbor across the street to do her grocery shopping. One day, out of the blue, she called her son and said, "I'm ready! Come and get me." It was as simple as that. People's thinking can change about staying in their home. Sometimes they realize that their house is just that, a house, and that they really don't need to be there anymore. Joyce said she was a loner, always had been and always would be, and that she wasn't going to get "roped in" to doing anything she didn't want to do when she moved. The next time we saw her at Beavers Acres, she had a bridge foursome and was serving cocktails and luncheon at noon. Many Seniors have a desire for more organized activities, a desire to meet new people or just to have contact with people.

Remaining in the home frequently requires employing either a part-time or full-time caregiver. Anyone who has ever had to find and keep a caregiver can understand how frustrating the process is. And that frustration is compounded when you have to start all over because someone you thought was good turns out to be abusing your parent, stealing from your parents, or basically not doing the job. Finding competent caregivers is one of the nightmares of your parents staying in their own homes. And even if you do find a good one and your parents become attached to her, she can just up and walk, leaving Mom and Dad more depressed than ever. When your friends start dying, your children move away, and your neighbor-hood begins to take a turn for the worse, it's time to think about relocating. If moving closer to your kids, friends, or siblings doesn't thrill you, try what Estelle did. She phoned her college Alumnae Office for a list of her classmates addresses and then wrote them a newsy letter, concluding with the idea that she'd like to move. Six months later, with a shoe box full of correspondence from old school pals, Estelle moved to Kalamazoo and her housemate is Earl, the friendly hasher from her sorority house.

Physical Layout of House and Neighborhood

Now that you've given some thought to whether you can afford to move, checked out your body for any new medical problems, and thought about who your new next best friend might be, it's time to consider how you could physically stay in your home if you became incapacitated, and to take a closer look at the direction your neigh-borhood is headed. What type of house do you live in? Is it a two story job or a ranch house? Is it level in or does it have a hundred stairs to walk up to ring the doorbell? Having good public transpor-tation close-by is crucial, especially if you no longer drive. If you don't drive, is there shopping within walking distance on flat streets where you won't have to worry about someone stealing your dinner? If your house is too large and your cleaning lady retired, the burden is on your shoulders. Do you really need a lot of room or does having a smaller place become more appealing as time goes on? If your home is two stories, is there a place you can make a bedroom and full bath on the first floor in case you are unable to get up the stairs at some point? Are the doors large enough for a wheelchair or walker and would being in a wheelchair make the kitchen counters too high? What about plugging in your old record player to listen to your Glen Miller albums—are they too low to bend down to reach?

A survey revealed that of all the Seniors' worries, the feeling of having no security in their own homes was their biggest fear. As we know, things never stay the same. Is your neighborhood as safe as it used to be? If not, why live there? Are your neighbors still the ones you've had for thirty years? How about being able to push that lawn mower? Has a new pastime become naming the different varieties of weeds in your yard? How about deciding you don't need the drawers filled with balls of string, twenty years of rubber bands, tops of jars (thousands of them), and closets full of plastic wrap from the cleaners, and what little old lady could toss shopping bags with handles?

Read the following checklist with your parents, and if they answer yes to seven, it's time to consider a move.

- If my mother fell, I doubt she could call for help.

- My parents don't travel because they worry about their home.

- My parents' neighborhood has gone downhill and I am concerned about their safety.

- There's no public transportation near my parents' home, and they're too cheap to call a cab.

▮ My parents live far from us and we don't always want to use our vacation time to visit them.

▮ My Dad's house is practically falling down because he's neglected to maintain it.

▮ Mom's social life is nil; she's nearly a recluse and complains about it all the time.

▮ It's becoming more difficult for Mom to shop and do her errands, so she watches Home Shopping Network and doesn't remember ordering three emerald necklaces.

▮ My parents are tired of taking care of themselves and they're slowly pushing more responsibility on me.

▮ Mom says she's eating well, but her garbage is full of Hostess Twinkies wrappers and cigarette butts.

▮ Dad always loved hot weather, but the air conditioner's been broken for a year, and he won't call a repair man.

▮ Mom's coming out of her shell since Dad died recently, and it would be great if she could meet some new people.

▮ Mom's not taking the right medications because there are too many for her to remember.

▮ Aunt Sophie's a worrier—she even worries whether the Girl Scouts will have the chocolate mint cookies next year.

■ Dad's leaving lighted cigarettes everywhere. He started a small fire and now the neighbors are concerned.

■ Mom won't listen to anything I have to say, so trying to talk to her about moving is a waste of time.

■ Sometimes I call four or five times a day and Mom doesn't answer because she forgets to put her hearing aid in. I'm afraid not to go over in case something has happened to her. This is a weekly scenario and it's getting boring.

■ Mother looks so sad and I know she feels isolated and lonely, but she doesn't say anything.

■ What will happen if Dad can't get to the doctor on his own?

■ We're having a hard time keeping competent caregivers at the house.

■ Taking care of Mom and Dad in their home has become a major problem for everyone involved.

■ I think my father has Alzheimer's because he doesn't re-member what a can opener is for.

■ Mom's running out of neighbors to help her.

■ My parents have friends that have moved to retirement communities and are surprised at how much they like them. It still doesn't help them budge.

4.

If I Decide to Move,
How Do I Choose the Right Place?

How do I find the right community?" is the single most asked question after someone has finally made the decision to move. There are two things to remember in choosing a community: First, after studying the brochures and visiting several communities, check to make sure you can meet the financial requirements and can pass the physical exam for entrance; and second, prioritize a list of your needs and wants, then go through your lists of communities and what they offer to pick a winner. Use the checklist at the end of the book to help facilitate your search. Spend some time in heart-to-hearts with the residents. The marketing director and administrator are trying to sell a product, and they may or may not be as candid with you as the residents. Keep your eyes and ears open, and take notes. When you visit retirement communities, take a camera and snap away, and when the photos are developed, write the name on the pack so you can re-visit in your mind. Ask a friend to accompany you when you check out various places—you'd be suprised what someone else notices. And remember—two heads are better than one.

Before investigating whether you get saltines with your soup, there are some things you should know. It's important for Seniors to have a sense of financial security concerning their choice of a living situation. You also should know if the community is a non-profit

or a for-profit community, as many non-profits will subsidize their residents. If you are a couple moving in, make sure you ask about the additional cost for the second person. Many people fail to understand that there is an additional cost and are shocked when they get their first bill with an extra seven or eight hundred dollars on it. Ask to have a list of the past annual increases in the monthly assessment so you can determine the average increase per year. You might not be able to move in if you are on a fixed income. Find out exactly what is and isn't included in the monthly assessment, because most likely there will be extras. If there is any doubt, it will probably cost you. On the brighter side, many places offer incentives to convince people to move in. The inducement can be as much as three month's free rent.

Most people list affordable cost, availability of health care, good food, compatible people, services and amenities, security, and location as the top seven concerns in choosing their new home. If you're buying into a community be sure you retain a lawyer or someone who understands retirement community contracts before signing anything. So many people wish they had asked more questions before moving.

Here are a few questions you should ask about the community itself:

■ How old is it?

■ Is it a rental or buy-in?

■ Does it have a religious affiliation?

■ What's the average age and is there a minimum or maximum age?

■ What are the physical requirements to enter?

■ Must a prospective resident pass a physical exam and, if so, must he use the community's doctor or can he use his own?

■ Does the community offer any long term care insurance and what kind of shape must you be in to qualify?

■ Are there any conditions under which a long term care insurance policy wouldn't cover a resident?

■ Can I use my own long term care policy?

■ Must you have Medicare to enter?

■ Is there an entrance fee or deposit, and is it refundable?

■ How many units are there and what is the number of residents?

■ What is the ratio of men to women?

- What is the average physical condition of the residents?

- Assuming there is a waiting list, how long is it and for which apartments?

- Does the community take SSI?

- Does the community subsidize residents?

- Is it accredited?

Again, visit as many communities as possible. The feeling of the place must appeal to you or it's not a fit. In the real-estate business, the saying goes that a home must have curb appeal to hook the potential buyer. The same test applies to a retirement community. And while you're checking everything out, find out about potential land use if there is any vacant land adjacent to the community. What, if any, are the future building plans and what is permitted in the area? Your field of dreams today might be tomorrow's parking lot or high rise. The following is a sampling of our checklist. It should give you enough ammunition to make a decision.

- Exterior atmosphere and condition.

- Type of building (high rise, clusters, cottages).

- Appeal of interior entrance.

- Attitude and behavior of staff.

- Attitude, appearance and behavior of residents.

▌ Dining: dress code, number of meals offered, assigned seating, service style or cafeteria, private dining room, parties catered, buffets, flexible dining hours, fixed menus or choices of food, salad bar, big meal in middle of day or in evening, substitutes available, snacks between meals, dietary and religious needs considered, meals appetizing and of sufficient quantity, wine served at dinner, guest meals available, fresh flowers on tables, separate assisted care dining, complimentary meals, and, last but not least, wheelchairs and walkers allowed in dining area?

▌ Alcohol and smoking policy in rooms, a smoking area or not at all?

▌ Location and climate.

▌ Public and private transportation.

▌ Accessibility to churches, shopping centers, and hospitals.

▌ Parking: Secure parking, indoor or outdoor, handicapped, visitor, and valet.

▌ Fitness and recreational activities.

▌ Amenities nearby.

- Activity areas available in the building.

- Social activities and gatherings.

- Presentations and planned activities and classes.

- Excursions and trips (extra charge?)

- Living arrangements: physical layout, maintenance and repairs.

- Individual unit features: individual temperature controls, air-conditioning, fireplaces in rooms, type and size of unit, gas or electric, carpeting and draperies included, adequate storage and closets, deck or patio, full kitchen or no oven, washer and dryer in unit, linens provided (no charge), (personal) laundry service available, housekeeping (how often and what does it entail?), tub and shower combination or shower only.

- Safety features: grab bars, electronic security system, emergency call system, pull cords, smoke detectors, indoor sprinklers, intercom system, safety check for residents, security officers.

- Medical services on premises or nearby.

- Assisted care section.

- Skilled nursing section.

- Alzheimer's wing.

▐ Physicians on call, on staff, do they make house calls, or not at all.

▐ LVNs or RNs on premises, weekly basis or not at all.

▐ Miscellaneous features and options:
>   24 hour on-site management,
>   Reciprocal use of facilities,
>   Guest room accommodations,
>   Free apartment on trial basis,
>   Beauty/barber shop,
>   Store/gift shop,
>   Chapel, library, video rentals, cleaners, bank.

▐ Pets allowed (on which floors, must you carry the pet to and from your unit, and are you able to replace the pet if it dies?)

You may need to personalize this list, thinking about your lifestyle and what's important to you. You may not get everything you want in one community, but make sure your highest priorities are met. After all, this will be your new home and you want to be as comfortable as possible.

5.
Housing Options for Seniors

Most older people want to stay put. They're reluctant to give up their homes and lifestyles of many years because they're comfortable in the neighborhood, and secure in the knowledge that they're close to familiar businesses and close friends. So for you who don't want to move from your surroundings, and for you who are thinking of moving, we'll explain some of the housing and living arrangements you might want to consider if you or your parents are adamant about not going to a structured retirement facility. There's no common nomenclature in our country when it comes to housing options for Seniors. A boarding house in West Virginia is called a Seniors Retirement Residence in Salt Lake City, and your father's trailer in Lexington, Kentucky, might be similar to his brother's in California, but there it's referred to as accessory housing. So while this is by no means a complete list of all the alternatives, and the names might vary, here's a sampling of some of the tried and true choices.

Manufactured Mobile Homes: These have become an increasingly attractive choice for older people. Today's models, some designed specifically for Seniors, are affordable, energy efficient, spacious, and loaded with extras that appeal to Grampa, such as specially adapted stove/oven dials for arthritic hands. You can choose the kind with wheels that can be moved, as the "snowbirds" who migrate from colder areas to warmer places do, or the roomy jobs that take a large truck to haul. Fees at Senior mobile home communities are moderate, many have activities and on-site services, and revised state and federal laws offer consumer protection not available until recently. If you live in a rural area, you might consider putting a trailer on your property for your parents, if zoning ordinances permit.

Cooperatives: Usually found in urban areas, this option combines most of the benefits of home ownership with the convenience and efficiency of multi-family housing. It is an option for the elderly who are willing to work cooperatively with other owners. This appeals to those who want to build equity in their accommodations, but don't want the isolation or responsibility of a larger home. Many are non-profit corporations that own and operate living facilities for the occupant's benefit, and people buy shares in the corporation in exchange for the right to occupy a specific unit. They are controlled by state laws which can vary widely, so seek good counsel who can advise you about all the angles before committing to anything.

Condominiums: While this type of ownership offers real advantages to older people, the style of life differs sharply from life in conventionally owned single family homes or rental apartments. For example, when to paint or fix the gutters is no longer your decision. You'll be housed in an apartment building or detached townhouse in which individuals hold title to their living unit, but share ownership of the common elements with all other owners. These common areas refer to utility buildings, grounds, swimming pools, etc. A dilemma arises for Seniors when the apartment building they've called home is converted to condominiums. For long-time renters, the conversion process can be disruptive and stressful. Many cities have ordinances requiring conversion landlords to continue renting to older tenants, so it might be just the ticket for you. But there are pitfalls; you'll need to figure out if the price of the unit and down payment are reasonable, is the basic structure sound, will the developer permit owners to offer their units for rent after purchase, and will condo fees for the first year of operation be sufficient to pay costs? As condos operate under state laws, we can't stress enough the need to seek legal and financial counsel before jumping in.

Accessory Apartments: These are a logical answer for many who've lived in a large house, but now find the unused space, utility bills, taxes and maintenance a nuisance. An accessory apartment is a second, completely private living unit created in the extra space of a single family home. There are a lot of pluses here, if the situation is right. Your widowed mother would have the security and companionship of someone living nearby, some additional income, and often tenants are willing to exchange services for rent reduction. The economic feasibility of creating an extra unit depends mainly on the house's design. We knew an 86-year old woman who had a contractor friend add an apartment in the attic in exchange for letting him move in for a year. She's able to stay in her house, doesn't worry about break-ins or being alone in an emergency, and can travel without the worry of leaving a home unattended. Again, check zoning ordinances thoroughly. Don't rely on verbal responses and get everything in writing.

ECHO Housing: This is an abbreviation of Elder Cottage Housing Opportunity, also called Granny Flats. The Senior housing dilemma has been lessened with ECHO houses which are separate, self-contained units designed for temporary installation in the side or backyard of an adult child's home. According to AARP, "It's a concept that permits closeness without sacrificing self-reliance." If zoning restrictions in your town prohibit ECHO housing, consider applying for a special use permit, which will expire when the unit is no longer needed. They're illegal in some areas, so you'll have to do your homework. Remember that the farther you are from a major city, the less restrictive zoning is likely to be.

Home-matching programs: These are gaining in popularity as community leaders, legislators and the general public address the lack of adequate Senior housing. The idea is to provide a service (often for a fee) that specializes in matching people. Many emphasize Seniors' needs. They go by different names—in Los Angeles it's listed as Housing Alternatives for Seniors. Start by asking Elder Care Case Managers and attorneys near you, or looking in the yellow pages under Elder, Housing or Seniors. When it works, it's a win/win situation, as it can enable an older person to stay in his house, and often it relieves the feelings of isolation and loneliness that many older people experience. Homesharing services report that the people who contact them usually are experiencing some sort of trauma in their lives such as facing a huge rent increase, being advised to give up driving, illness, or tremendous grief over loss of a spouse. This emotional strain is one of the reasons why sponsoring groups train staff and volunteers to counsel, as well as to be homefinders. A good home-matching service offers counseling to prospective applicants to help them identify their needs and pinpoint their doubts, as shared housing isn't for everyone. Most adults are used to setting the house rules, and being in charge of one's domicile, so new restrictions and lists of things that are off-limits seem ridiculous. Whether you're the homeowner or the one looking for a place to hang your hat, you should make a decision only after you've carefully weighed the pros and cons. At the very least you should spend a trial week to see if the honeymoon would last.

If you can't find a program with counseling, and resort to the old "well-it-sounds-OK" method, ask a friend or relative to help you answer a few basic questions about yourself, as another person can often be more objective. Questions such as: Am I fairly flexible, adaptable to change? Am I able to express how I feel honestly? Can I admit my frailties and shortcomings? Am I relatively tolerant of others' feelings and behavior?

If you have to wrestle with the above considerations, home-sharing might not be for you. On the other hand, you might find someone with whom you'd click, and we all know people who've stayed together when no one thought they'd last more than a month. One home-matching program suggested both parties make a list of "Ten Things Other People Do That Drive Me Nuts" which they could share with potential housemates. Here's their prize sample:

1. People who always lose things, "I can't find my glasses."
2. Drivers who get irate and yell at other motorists.
3. People who complain about their ailments—the limit is one complaint per day.

4. Anybody with no hobbies, interests or recreational activities.

5. People who are too tight to pay for the paper and think they can sneak in my yard and read mine before I get up.

6. Friends who sit down to watch TV and snore so loud the canary quits singing.

7. When my grandson uses the last toilet paper and then goes out to build a snow fort.

8. People who don't clean up their dishes and who belch at the supper table.

9. Friends who don't remember that I can't remember everything.

10. People who can't spare some kindness.

Obviously if you're a couch potato who gets up to sneak the paper, then snores, belches and crabs about your health after you've left dirty dishes around and finished off the toilet paper, you won't have much in common with this woman who was hoping to find someone to live with her. The good news is that she might not remember.

Shared Housing, or, "We Did It In College, Why Not Try It Now?" This is what the TV sitcom *The Golden Girls* was all about, and wasn't it a barrel of laughs? The benefits of this type of arrangement can be numerous. It can be economical, it can provide companionship, as living together often helps overcome loneliness, and think of the sense of security it provides. And socially, a peer support system is what we all hope for. But it's certainly not for everyone, so re-appraise your expectations, lighten up and hope your new roommate is Blanche. As in the above matching service, you'll have to be specific about what you are offering if you're the landlord, and be as candid and questioning as possible if you're hoping to move in with someone else. We know a woman who rents three bedrooms in her spacious house to other women, and she asks prospective tenants to rate themselves on the Felix and Oscar cleanliness scale, going from 1 to 10.

Remember, your options will be determined largely by your checkbook, the state of your health, your support system, and to a large part, your attitude. You'll want to consider many things you never dreamed would be important, but it's no time to be timid—go ahead and ask if you can play your harmonica at midnight. If you are looking for a renter, take a photograph of your place, and spell out in writing exactly what the arrangements will be, what's negotiable and what's cast in stone. Do your homework and be clear about your policies concerning pets, overnight guests, smoking, and who does what in the kitchen. A couple who have been renting rooms to Seniors for years told us the chances are good if a prospective tenant's lived in a fraternity house, been in the military, or gone to summer camp and survived. You'll need to find out about a few things: Do you need a business license? Does your homeowner's insurance cover renters? Will you be reporting the income? Will neighbors complain about extra cars? Can you take deductions on your income taxes if you're renting? And can you get that look of disgust off your puss when your new tenant's slurping fudge sauce on you brand new ecru sofa and her teeth are soaking in your Waterford vase?

Adult Foster Care: Also called Adult Family Homes, Adult Foster Care is provided in a private home occupied by an indvidual or family who offers room, meals, housekeeping, and generally minimal supervision and personal care for a monthly fee. Don't confuse these homes with "Board and Cares" which fall under more stringent licensing in most states. Staff cannot administer medications in adult foster care homes unless he/she is a nurse, which is precisely why so many are operated by nurses.

Retirement Hotels, also called Senior Residence Hotels, Residential Hotels for Seniors, and Retirement Residences. This is a confusing area because in some cities these are called Senior apartments, but here's what we found in several urban areas. Guidelines state they are intended for people over 62, although some take younger tenants with mental and physical disabilities. These domiciles come in every price range, architectural form and environment imaginable. One resident told us finding a suitable one was comparable to looking for the right woman, "you have to shop carefully and one will just feel right." Some are high-rises around landscaped gardens, others are drab concrete shoe boxes, but they're good locations with good public transportation. Make a list of what's important to you. Tenants usually have a choice of private or semi-private room, private or shared bath. Some complexes offer nothing more than a room and bath, others sport putting greens and espresso bars. Rent can include three meals daily, maid service five days a week, 24-hour desk service, and an activities program, field trips, card rooms, beauty shops, and a daily cocktail hour. If a resident needs help with personal grooming or chores, the staff knows who's available for a fee, and if you prefer, you can rent another room for your companion and they'll waive the "over 62 rule." These places generally don't have kitchens in the rooms, but you could bring a microwave and small refrigerator. Be sure to check out the wheelchair policy if it's of concern to you.

Boarding House. This is basically renting a room, sometimes shared, in someone else's house, with a manager on the premises.

Seniors Apartment House. Some of these monthly rentals have security systems, vans to transport residents, activities, and a full complement of amenities; others offer lodging only.

The bottom line is to be clear about your needs. Make a list, beginning with how much you can afford, and consider trade-offs such as giving up your car and taking taxis, and using the extra money on something you really like. Wilma wanted the bedroom opening onto the garden at Hilary's Haven, as it recalled memories of her rose-growing days. She finally took a room overlooking the parking lot, covered the walls with prints of prize-winning gardens, and is able to visit her grandchildren in Chagrin Falls twice as often on what she saved.

No wonder we're confused—looking under *Homes for the Elderly* in the San Francisco yellow pages, one finds this diverse selection:

Alice's Care Home
Angela's Rest Home
Andrews Boarding and Care Home
Barcelona Residential Care Home
Belen's Residential Care Home For the Elderly
Bernal Heights Retirement Home
Best House for Elderly Care
Bridget's Care Center
Bryant Daisy Rest Home
Gabriel's Home for the Ambulatory Aged
Janet's Residential Facility for the Elderly
Lina's Guest Home
May's Love and Care Home
Mercy Retirement and Care Center
Oakcreek Alzheimer's and Dementia Care Center
Pacific Heights Manor
Robert Frost Retirement Center
University Mound Ladies Home

We know they're pushing love and care at May's, and Angela hints at rest while Lina wants us to feel like a guest—the only listing that actually spells out the problems that will be addressed is the Alzheimer's Care Center. One can see common nomenclature doesn't exist in the board and care industry today. We telephoned most of the places, ascertained that fluency in English wasn't a requirement to be working there, and determined that most of the listings fell under the guidelines of Board and Care facilities. States license board and care homes under more than 25 different names, so make sure you know in what capacity the facility you are looking at is licensed.

6.

Adapting the House to Meet the Seniors' Needs

T here are few things in life more devastating than having to move from your home because it no longer fits your needs. When one can't provide for himself in the manner to which he's accustomed, and can no longer do the things he used to do around the house, then one of the options is to remodel the house so he can stay. As people age, the senses change, the vision and hearing became less acute, and the sense of smell starts to go. The greatest fear Seniors' seem to have is falling and breaking a bone, or not being able to get up. We can not reverse our aging process but it is possible to adapt to these changes.

Staying in your home is an option many Seniors choose. One of the problems with this decision is that the Senior and his family do not prepare the home for the older adult's future needs. If you have 75 stairs to your front porch, this is not a workable situation, or if you don't know how to use those new hearing aids or just simply forget to put them in, you could get into some real trouble. Sally kept losing her hearing aids and the family was getting a little upset as each pair cost about $1,500. She had been caring for her frail husband but was starting to get just a little weary from all the responsibility. One morning she forgot to put her hearing aids in and her husband slipped in the bathroom and cut his head. He lay there for almost an hour, lost quite a bit of blood, and when she found him she had to rush him to the hospital. This is a sign to the family that a move should be considered. Let's talk a little about some of the physical problems that Seniors might have to face, and what they can do in order for them to continue living independently in their own homes.

Vision loss: Vision loss increases after the age of 65, and almost one out of every 20 people over 85 is legally blind. With vision loss, one of the most important changes you need to make to your home is the lighting. Seeing objects clearly and moving from light to dark areas are where the most accidents occur. Placement of furniture and solid color flooring (you need differentiation in the color) are two other ways of ameliorating this problem.

Hearing loss: Some degree of hearing loss is the most common disability among Seniors. Using volume enhanced telephones, amplified TV sets, louder doorbells, and making sure the smoke detectors are loud enough, will all help the hearing impaired live with more ease in their own home. An intercom system can be vital if one spouse is caring for another who is ill. Window coverings and wall to wall carpet help to reduce the background noise.

Arthritis: This is a common aliment with Seniors. The serious problems are gripping kitchen knobs, doorknobs, buttoning clothes and using kitchen utensils. They need to use controls, knobs, and levers that will enable them to open and close doors, turn on the kitchen and baths faucets, and open drawers. Blinds can be a problem too, so putting a larger pull knob on the cord helps. There are even battery operated shades and screens available.

Balance: Dizziness and disorientation can greatly affect our balance as we age, so getting rid of years of accumulation can create a safer environment. Pathways should be clear. Handrails in halls and stairs, and grab bars in the bath areas must be installed. Try to use furniture without sharp edges. Even though taping scatter rugs sounds like a good idea, it usually is only temporary. How about just getting rid of them?

Mobility Impairment: Loss of the ability to move around with the same ease as before is a huge problem. Getting up and down stairs, in and out of the tub, up and down from furniture, and in and out of a car all take much more time and energy and strength than it used to. Being in a wheelchair most of the time makes the remodeling of the home even more necessary. Even though parents might not need to remodel at the present time, a time will come when that need may arise. If you do decide to do a little work, you might consider even more.

Here are some suggestions, room by room, that might help you in planning a remodel job for your aging parents.

Kitchen

- Use handle pulls with an opening, not knobs.

- Make sure linoleum is in good condition in the kitchen. Catching a shoe on an edge is a common occurrence for older adults.

- If there are thresholds between rooms, be sure the edges are leveled or remove them.

- Install lever-type faucets on sinks or a touchless water faucet.

- Use burners that turn off automatically.

- If confined to a wheelchair, lower the kitchen cabinets and create a space below the sink for the wheelchair.

- Use rounded edges on the counter tops rather than sharp to reduce injury.

- Use knife guards.

- Put signs in the kitchen reminding you to turn off the stove.

- Choose a counter top color that contrasts with the floor.

- Use a side by side refrigerator/freezer.

- Plugs should be high enough so that Seniors don't have to bend down.

- Switch for the disposal should be on the front of the sink.

- Open shelving for food or a walk-in pantry is helpful.

- Use revolving shelves for easy access.

- Keep combustibles away from heat.

- Keep cookware with handles turned away from the edge of the stove.

- Check for grease build-up around exhaust duct or hood, broiler, burners, and oven.

- Keep poisons in a secure place and marked with an X.

- Have a fire extinguisher handy and in working order. Make sure it is one that will work on grease fires.

- Check gas stoves for any leaks.

- Have Ground Fault Interrupters installed.

Living room and dining room

- If there are smokers, have a smoking area with plenty of ashtrays. It is very dangerous for older persons to be walking around the house smoking. And never smoke in your bed.

▊ Use darker color flooring and lighter draperies. Always use contrasting colors so you can differentiate between chairs, stools, plates on tables, tablecloths etc.

▊ Make sure the lighting is uniform with no glare.

▊ Keep floors free of clutter.

▊ Remove cords running across a room, and try not to tape them down. It is preferable to run them up over the doors or move the furniture closer to the walls.

▊ Make sure heavy items such as televisions and stereos are fixed in place or out of the way.

▊ Have furniture that is high enough.

▊ Use furniture that has arms and firm padding in the seats.

▊ Chairs with casters help in the dining area, as well in the room watching TV.

▊ If buying a recliner, make sure you can get out of it. You might consider the kind with an ejection button if you like the idea of being shot out of a cannon.

▊ Remove any unnecessary furniture in the room.

Bathroom

▊ Hot water heaters should be set to control the heat of the water.

▋ Have non-skid surfaces in showers and tubs.

▋ Shower glass doors should be shatter-proof or use a shower curtain.

▋ Buy an elevated toilet, or use a portable or adjustable one to put over the existing toilet.

▋ Have a (GFI) ground fault interrupter installed in the bath.

▋ Use lever hands in sink and shower, or the single lever type in the shower and tub.

▋ Sink height is important for clearance if a wheelchair is involved. Also remove the doors to the existing cabinet or remove the cabinet and install an open cabinet.

▋ Tub and shower seats are important if it is difficult for the Senior to stand for long periods of time or if they have a problem with balance.

▋ Non-skid tiles or adhesive on the bathroom floors helps with any moisture and prevents slipping.

▋ You can never have too much lighting in a bathroom, so use as many lights as possible, but avoid glare, which makes seeing difficult.

▋ Storage should be accessible from a wheelchair as well as standing.

▍ Always have a night-light in the bath as well as in the hall leading to the bath.

▍ A manual as well as an overhead shower head is good.

Bedroom

▍ Night-light should be on in the bedroom at night.

▍ Make sure bed height is appropriate for your condition.

▍ Have a clear and uncluttered path to the bathroom.

▍ Single beds are easier to use and make, especially if one of the partners is ill.

▍ Have good lighting next to the bed to safeguard against falls and to make reading in bed a pleasure.

▍ If hard of hearing, use a phone jack to connect light to phone so the light will blink when phone rings.

▍ Use tight short carpeting for the whole house, but especially in the rooms that are used the most.

▍ Poles in closets should be lowered, shoes raised, and using open shelving for most clothes is helpful. Sometimes a closet consultant can work wonders.

Living in the house

▍ Have emergency numbers in all rooms.

▌ Have flashlights and extra batteries in all rooms, maybe even installed on the wall of each room.

▌ Make doors larger by replacing hinges or enlarging opening if needed for wheelchairs.

▌ Keep furnace filters clean.

▌ Have first aid kits in kitchen and baths.

▌ Create a bedroom with a full bath on the first floor if you have a two story house.

▌ Have hand railings on both sides of the stairs and in the halls

▌ Have very tight carpeting on the stairs or no carpeting at all.

▌ Use non-skid strips if the floor is bare.

▌ Put peepholes in the front door, one low and one high.

▌ Have a plan for exiting your home in case of an emergency.

▌ Make sure fire extinguishers work.

▌ Do a safety tour of your home before you remodel.

▌ Consider buying a "Life Line" system so if you fall, you can get help.

▌ Install smoke detectors in every room.

▌ Have good lighting throughout the house.

∎ Install a pet door if Bowser is still around.

∎ Install automatic garage door openers with lights that go on when you drive in and stay on until you get inside.

∎ Use Halogen lights wherever you can.

Outside

∎ If you have wooden stairs going to a yard, check to see if there are any nails sticking up which could cause you to trip.

∎ Build a ramp for wheelchair accessibility.

∎ Have hoses installed safely and never leave them across a path.

∎ Have adequate outdoor lighting especially in areas that are concealed from the street, and be sure they are working. Sensor lights work well.

∎ Remove any obstructions on walkways.

∎ Place non-skid tape that is a different color on the stairs going up to the house.

∎ Wind breaks on the decks and patios should be shatter proof.

∎ Repair uneven bricks or cement on patios and walkways.

∎ Repair exposed electrical wiring or unsafe outlets on the exterior of the house.

Protection

Now that you have refitted your home so you will be able to live in it if your physical needs change, you will want to consider the safety aspect of living at home. As we know, older adults are often victims of serious crimes, so you will want to deter anyone from breaking into your home.

■ Get a good alarm system that is easy to use and plaster signs all over the front of your house.

■ Cut away shrubery and bushes from around the house.

■ Put bars on windows on lower levels, but ones that can be opened from the inside.

■ Join a neighborhood watch group.

■ Double bolt all doors.

■ Have good flood lights pointed at areas that are dark.

■ Sliding doors should have double locks.

■ Windows should stay locked when not being used.

■ Make friends with your neighbors so they know your routine.

■ Contact the group called YANA (You Are Not Alone) and find out what they can do for you. Get on their list.

■ Don't go out late at night alone.

Other than the physical remodeling of your home, there are other factors that make staying there more appealing. Try going to a Senior Center in your neighborhood. Meals on Wheels and other for-profit meal services are springing up everywhere. Most offer very tasty and well prepared meals. Having Medicare therapy in your home is a plus and remember, if you are not well enough to go to a Senior Center, try an adult day care center for some interaction with people and get a good meal at the same time. One of the major hurdles you will face is living in a home with lots of stairs. If that is the case, you may have to consider an elevator or, if worse comes to worse, move to a single-level home. It can make or break the difference in your lifestyle.

7.
Planned Adult Communities

Planned Adult Communities sprang up after Del Webb's Sun City was a runaway success in the fifties in Arizona. Retired snowbirds from the shivering northeast sought the warmth of the Sunbelt, they found new friends, and the concept took off. Today there are hundreds of these developments, primarily in warmer climates, and the more successful ones sell out soon after completion. Planned Adult Communities are characterized by clusters of apartments and condominiums or single family homes built around a core of services and amenities. Residents can own their property, and must abide by the Covenants, Codes and Restrictions administered by a governing body which deals with policies of the community facilities, property requirements, charges and assessments, and provisions of the association of homeowners. They're usually found on the outskirts of major cities—removed from the congestion and high real estate prices, and they promote a vision of healthy, active retirees enjoying their golden years in tranquil leisure. These communities, some of which are like manicured campuses, are great for couples and can be an ideal option for singles, as there is a built-in social system, loads of activities, and a sense of security that's reassuring to Seniors.

A typical community might be laid out around a couple of golf courses, surrounded by rolling hills, with tennis courts, pools, hiking and biking trails, and recreational facilities abounding. We visit-

ed one with lawn bowling, fly-casting ponds, drama center, exercise rooms and enough social activities to satisfy any debutante. It's difficult to determine how much it costs to buy into this type of community, as costs vary so greatly around the country, and one has to factor in amenities and services offered. As new phases are added to the original developments, it's possible to find a re-sale for a good price. We visited one with a membership entrance fee of $3,000, and another where it was $150, and an assortment of assessments, fees and extra charges seem to be common in these retirement havens.

Moving to a Senior planned community can be a good way to ease the transition from moving from the large family home to eventually going to an environment with more services. You can pare down gradually, or in phases, to suit yourself. In many ways, you have the best of all worlds because you can usually rent an apartment or house on a temporary basis, and you'll be able to see if you like the lifestyle. You might find that this type of living arrangement just isn't your cup of tea. If you love having kids around, like to hear teenagers' rock and roll, and you enjoy interaction among the generations, then you might want to skip this phase and stay in your home.

Take the responsibility yourself to find out what else the developer has built, and also be cautious about buying in an area with a lot of retirement communities. Is yours going to be half sold leaving you with property difficult to sell? Developers sometimes offer "perks" on unsold properties to move the real estate, meaning a house or unit will be offered at less than what you paid, thus devaluing your property. Usually you don't discover this until it's time to sell and you see the comparables. Don't think that you'll make money on this property and that you can rent your place and move somewhere else, because when you read the fine print in the contract you're likely to discover that you can usually rent for only one year. In most communities, you or your spouse must be 55, but get a load of what happened to Harold. Midge and he lived in Sherwood Forest for 11 years before she died. A year after her death Harold married a much younger woman with two teenagers, of whom Harold was quite fond. His soon-to-be-bride redecorated the house, even making a game room for the kids. Imagine Harold's shock when, after the honeymoon, he learned that according to the Covenants, Codes and Restrictions, his step-children couldn't live with them. He had to sell his house in a soft market, and buy a suitable place in suburbia, where lawn-mowing and snow-shoveling were his responsibility, and golf games with neighbors were hazy memories.

Don't be shy about asking questions during your visit; if one community doesn't appeal to you or offer what you're looking for, go on to the next. We found some communities with medical facilities on the premises, while at others, the doctors were nearby. It's up to you to:

- Read and understand the CC&Rs thoroughly or they'll return to haunt you. These tell you what you can and can't do to your dwelling.

- Ask the amount of the entrance fee and any other fees.

- Find out what the monthly assessment is.

- Inquire if there's an increase in the homeowners fee each year?

- What are the services that it covers?

- Find out, in addition to your monthly mortgage, what the yearly homeowner fee is.

- Ask if homeowners pay for anything extra?

- Determine what the governing body is, their responsibilities, and how long they serve.

- See if there is a restaurant on the premises.

- Ask where medical services are.

- Figure out how close shopping is.

- Find out if there is regularly scheduled transportation to shopping/medical facilities

▌ Find out what the policy on children staying in my home is.

▌ Ask what the largest and smallest unit available is.

▌ See if there are restrictions on cars, boats and RVs, if this pertains to you.

▌ Inquire whether there's an activities committee.

▌ Determine if you must pay anything to the community when you sell your place.

▌ Learn if there are any restrictions on recreational facilities, or are they for everyone's use at no additional cost?

▌ See if there's a security gate.

▌ Ask what the average age is.

▌ Find out how far the nearest emergency medical facility is.

▌ Inquire about medical services on the premises.

▌ Ask if the community provides transportation within the development.

▌ Obtain in writing whether or not you can retain your own agent to sell your unit.

8.

Independent Retirement Communities

W̲e think the phrase Independent Retirement Community is somewhat contradictory. When these communities opened they targeted a population that was active, self-reliant, and capable of living independently. However, as the residents aged, the fiber of the community began to change. Even though active Seniors continued to move in, some of those who had lived there longer needed more help. A community can't maintain a truly independent status when people begin to require assistance with activities of daily living.

This type of Senior living ranges from studios, cottages, and townhouses, to mid and high-rise apartment houses, some offering communal activities, security, a variety of meal plans, and other services. However, they don't include medical care. In many states, owners and operators aren't required to be licensed, nor are they subject to regulations and guidelines that apply to other types of communities. They can charge the public pretty much what the traffic will bear. An unlicensed community isn't required to offer anything other than meals. This means that virtually anyone can open an Independent Retirement Community and operate it any way he chooses. It's necessary to do your homework when considering this type of living arrangement, as they vary across the country, and it's not always clear what you are getting. We saw far too many caregivers in communities that billed themselves as Independent.

Just what did we see as we made the rounds? A good percentage of the facilities are attractive and well kept, with older adults enjoying a variety of amenities, a caring staff aware of the residents' changing needs, and a full complement of activities. Does this sound idyllic? All that glitters isn't gold.

We were shocked to find:

- Wheelchair-bound residents living on the third floor, and with only one elevator.

- A community of five floors with no sprinklers or smoke alarms.

- A building with a no wheelchairs in common areas rule, meaning that if you rely on a wheelchair, you are room-bound. Forget eating with your friends, playing bingo, or watching a ball game in the multi-purpose room.

- Vans that aren't handicapped-equipped; thus a trip to the doctor could cost hundreds of dollars without your insurance covering it.

- If you do have to take meals in your room, there is a service charge per tray, even though the rules stipulate that wheelchairs are forbidden in the dining room. None of this is mentioned in the brochure or discussed in the interview.

- Many communities lack full kitchens or even kitchenettes.

- Communities that forbid alcohol in your own room or apartment. On the other hand, we visited a place where the administration was installing an attractive bar to make the social events more convivial.

■ Communities that wouldn't let us talk to the residents.

Don't discount your intuition about a facility, because that initial feeling is usually the right one. Does it seem like a business, a hotel, or a home? The information below may help you in your choice. Residents can have private pay personal care and can supply their own. In many communities the staff knows reliable caregivers and will give you those names, others will not share their sources with you, as they are concerned about the liability of implied responsibility. Bringing up the topic of wheelchairs was like opening a can of worms. In general we found administrators didn't want to sound as if anyone was discriminating against wheelchairs. They implied it was the residents who didn't want to see them.

We were told incoming residents could not be in a wheelchair, but walkers were not frowned upon. As to who allows wheelchairs, we found this to be a very gray area, with no consistency. We heard variations of : "no," "only in their room," "yes, with assistance," "case by case," and just plain "yes". What happens to the person who needs a wheelchair after moving in? Sometimes it's up to the residents' council, sometimes it's perfectly OK, and in some places wheelchairs are forbidden in common areas. The truth of the matter is that administrators don't want prospective residents to think they're coming into a wheelchair swap meet. We couldn't understand why wheelchairs weren't permitted in the dining room. Did it interfere with their image of being an independent community or did it have something to do with the fire code? When we asked residents how they felt about it, the response was, "It's too depressing, this is a place for healthy people." We wondered after hearing this so many times, how these people would feel when and if it happened to them. It was unanimous. Nothing is written in the contract and the administrators told us they did not make a point of telling incoming residents. This is a fine state of affairs if you have made the big move and are later confined to a wheelchair. Wouldn't it be easier if the community spelled it out up front? We talked with a woman who was aware of the policy prior to her move. This astute Senior had a clause in her contract enabling her wheelchair-bound niece to join her in the dining room. We were told that the residents were far more accepting of their peers who deteriorate on site than the new person coming in with a disability.

Call us paranoid, but we were appalled to learn that in many of these facilities, which were all two and three stories, they did not meet fire codes. Only one had a sprinkler system. We talked with a fire inspector after hearing this. He said these buildings weren't required to be inspected because they weren't licensed by the state.

The majority of places admit people who already need assistance with personal care. The administrators want you to believe that only a small percentage of residents need assistance, but it contradicts what we saw. As we sat in the lobby of one of the more upscale Independent Retirement Communities, we counted 13 residents with caregivers in 15 minutes, and only two residents who looked able to make it to the dining room on their own steam. We compared leases in all the rental communities we visited and found that all were month-to-month, and the majority were pro-rated for fifteen days, meaning if you left on the sixteenth you lost money. The security deposit differed from place to place, with amounts ranging from zero to one thousand dollars, with lots of variables. Every community's policy differs. Inquire if fees are refundable or can be applied to the rent. Entrance fees vary, and every facility required a first month's rent up front. A lot of these communities do not have a financial statement for prospective residents to see. Many are privately owned, and the owners don't want to divulge this information, so you need to do some sleuthing on your own. How long has Cherry Acres been in business? Is it part of a chain? We would look twice if it's only six months old, will not give you a financial statement, and isn't affiliated with a reputable group. Yearly rent increases range from two to nine per cent. This is where you, the adult child, and you, the parent, need to be on the ball. Very few administrators admitted they told residents there would be a rental increase. When we asked why they didn't forewarn residents, the response was loud and clear. They simply were not asked. Because the general public is not informed in advance, and because it's not in the contract, down the line your parents may not be able to afford this community if on a fixed or limited income.

Edna, who had been a CPA, did ask about the increase each

year, and was told that in the past it had averaged between two and three per cent. She wanted to live in a high-end community which was a little more than she could afford, but figured she could manage for ten years, because by then she'd be one hundred. The year after she moved in, the administration raised the rent by eight percent, leaving good-natured Edna worrying constantly about her future. It doesn't happen often that a resident can't pay, but if it occurs, the resident wouldn't be able to stay, as most private rental communities do not subsidize residents. We know there are exceptions to this, but don't count on it. All said they would give the resident adequate time to find new housing.

Just about everyone allows pets, but be sure to ask if your St. Bernard is welcome. Most rentals require a pet deposit and some stipulate that you live on the first floor. Be prepared for the question, "Who will care for your Sparky if something happens to you or if you go on vacation?" Some communities even have a policy stating if you can't carry your pet outside, you can't have one.

If you must go into a nursing facility, as long as you are paying the rent, the apartment is yours. They will, however, prorate your rent and take out the food costs. If it appears you may be out more than three months, most will recommend that you give up your apartment and move back in later.

Surprisingly, for independent communities, most require that you take three meals a day. However, the a la carte system is becoming more popular. Don't count on making those holiday cookies, as most communities we visited didn't have ovens in the kitchens. Does this spell independence to you?

In past years smoking was allowed; however, with today's concerns about safety and smoking's effects, many communities have changed their policies to allow smoking in your own room, in a designated common area, or outside. As for alcohol, that's a question to ask. Why shouldn't you be able to have a pop at 5 o'clock in your own room?

If you've decided to make the move to an Independent Retirement Community, here are some additional points to keep in mind:

■ Visit several and be sure to take a tour of the entire community.

■ Is there a time limit grandchildren can stay?

■ Ask if they have a complimentary apartment so you can test the waters.

■ Ask for a copy of the lease and read it carefully.

■ Talk to both the administrator and the marketing director. You may get two different viewpoints.

■ Observe and talk to the residents. Do they seem content?

▌ Have a meal and check out the choices.

▌ Attend an activity or two.

▌ Is there private transportation?

▌ Is there an emergency alert system?

▌ How close is it to shopping and medical facilities?

▌ What's included in the rent?

▌ Is there assigned seating in the dining room?

▌ Do apartments have individual temperature controls?

▌ If I decide to be gone for an extended period, can I rent my apartment?

▌ Sniff around and we do mean sniff. Trust your nose!

The Independent Retirement Community may be the Edsel of the Senior Housing Industry, conceived and designed for the active Senior, forgetting they will age. Coupled with the trend to wait to move into a community until you have to, the future for these facilities, we believe, will be as Assisted Living. We visited some extremely attractive communities offering independent living—from those with manicured gardens, enticing amenities, and cocktail parties, to dreary, renovated city apartments. All these communities fulfill a need, but you should be open-minded and diligent as you search for the right one. It all bears planning ahead.

9.
Rental Communities with Two, Three, and Four Levels of Care

R|ental communities with more than one level of care have mushroomed in the last ten years. Developers saw there was a need to fill as well as money to be made. With the aging of our population, many people who are now living longer are faced with the inevitable truth that they can't stay in their homes living the quality of life they had been experiencing. For this reason, many have chosen to move. "Why move to a rental community?" is a question we are asked frequently. There are many reasons, the most common being: "I don't want to own anything anymore, I want flexibility in my living situation, it's a good way to try a community without a major commitment, my health or my partner's health may be failing," and lastly, "for financial considerations."

Older people don't want to or can't tie up their cash, or they may not have enough money to come up with a lump sum to buy into a community. So it's important to familiarize yourself with the choices offered in rental communities at each level, as there could be financial, emotional, and medical repercussions if you make the wrong choice. The Epstein's really liked the ambiance of the Westgate but it was billed as just an independent community. With Mr. Epstein's health beginning to fail, they had expressed to their family how strongly they felt about being separated, so when they picked the Westgate over a community with three levels of care everyone was surprised. As Murphy's law would have it, within three months Mrs. Epstein fell and had to be moved into a skilled nursing facility three miles from the Westgate. Shortly thereafter she developed pneumonia and died. How sad that Mr. Epstein, due to his physical condition, was unable to visit his wife at a time when they should have been together. A better choice of a community would have saved them this anguish.

The services and amenities in these communities run the gamut from sparse and dreary to opulent. It all depends on who's running the show. That's why we encourage you to visit as many as possible for comparison, and to spend the night and eat the food at the places that put a smile on your face.

The communities that offer two levels of care seem to be the most common. These places grew out of the need for independent facilities to accommodate the Seniors as they grew older and needed additional care. In some locations these two levels are integrated but in most they are segregated. This is a very important point to address when shopping for rentals. If the community has a policy of segregation, this usually means that the residents living in the assisted living section have their own wing of the building, their own dining room, and sometimes their own activities. The apartments can be smaller than in independent living and in most cases there is no stove or burner in the kitchenette. This can affect couples more than singles, as one of the couple who may not be impaired in any way is still forced to be in the assisted living wing. There are a few places that would let people in assisted living use the main dining room, but in general this isn't the case. If the healthy partner doesn't want to be in the assisted living wing, then he would have to pay an additional monthly fee to stay in his independent unit. It would be nice if you could have your own private pay caregiver come into the independent living section to care for a partner, but again most of the communities didn't permit it. The logic of this is in the licensing and can also be at the discretion of the operators. If the owner licenses his entire building as assisted living it can cost much more than if he does only a section of the building. You need to be aware of the downside and be armed with appropriate questions so your parents and you will understand what you are getting into.

In response to the growing need for even more extended care in rental communities, we now have three, four and even five levels of care within one facility. The third level is the Skilled Nursing, the fourth an Alzheimer's unit, and the fifth an adult day care center for Seniors living outside the community. These are all concepts which have given the older adult a feeling of security in being able to stay in one place and not having to move again. And, if you are a couple, it affords you the luxury of being close to your loved one. But pay attention and stay alert. You are not necessarily guaranteed a place in the skilled nursing facility and some of the communities are not approved for Medicare, which means if you are counting on Medicare to help pay your costs, you are out of luck. Some of the things we were told off the record were: they can't tell you wheelchairs are not allowed, you can not be forced into taking a physical exam, some of the units in some of the communities are subsidized, and they said a good question to ask was how often a person was turned down when they needed to move to a new level of care, because the community had taken too many people from the outside directly into the higher levels.

One of the first questions we would ask a community was what do you call yourself. There is no uniformity in naming types of communities throughout the country. We were given various names such as a Full Service Retirement Community, and A Continuum of Care Community.

A very important question to ask in all levels of rentals is, "Can you supply your own caregivers and can you have those caregivers come to your independent unit?" At the two level community, residents could have private pay personal care and could supply their own. So, if this is important to you, ask and get it in writing. The difference in cost in supplying your own and using one from the facility can sometimes add up to a large piece of change. Even if a community will let you have your own caregiver, don't hold your breath for them to recommend one to you. They usually don't as this can imply responsibility in the quality of care given. Remember, most places do their own evaluation upon entering and can re-evaluate you at any time, sometimes adding additional charges for extra care without letting the family know. Check your bills carefully every month.

Allowing wheelchairs in the independent living sections of these communities is a hotbed of dissension and again a very gray area with no consistency. Even though the Americans with Disabilities Act states that a person in a wheelchair can not be discriminated against, you would be surprised at the number of places that still try and get around it. One manager stressed that safety was his prime concern, thus he allowed wheelchairs only on the first floor. What happens when a person on the third floor needs a wheelchair? Must he move? About half the communities even came right out and said that they did not allow wheelchairs in the dining room, and only a few allowed walkers. Administrators told us the residents had voted on a "no wheelchair policy." What surprised us was that these same sweet little old ladies and gentlemen would not address the issue of themselves being in that same position some day. It's called denial.

Communities should allow wheelchairs and walkers everywhere if the building meets the fire codes. It's part of the aging process, it's reality, and it's inconsistent with the philosophy of graceful aging. As for wheelchairs in the dining room, this issue caused a big stink whenever we asked the question. Most of the communities said they discouraged it, while others just came right out and said no. Imagine if both your parents lived at Los Arroyos and Mom was in a wheelchair, they would have to eat in separate dining rooms if Dad didn't want to go to the assisted living section to eat. We also had Stephanie tell us her daughter with MS was refused entrance into the dining room because she was in a wheelchair. It's a pretty stiff rule. Don't be bullied. You're on the side of the law!

The issue of separating people in assisted living and independent living in the dining areas is a sensitive subject and one that stirs much emotion. One can understand intellectually that there might be times when it would be appropriate, especially when the resident is embarrassed by his or her condition, but in general it seems a little archaic. Most of the communities did have separate dining rooms, but we found very few enlightened facilities with a healthy approach to this somewhat sticky wicket. Their philosophy, which we rather liked, is that segregating people based on their infirmities somehow undermines one's dignity, and that things are tough enough at this age without having to feel a sense of isolation and rejection. Why take away what little independence and control these folks have left? A good solution would be to have two dining rooms and let the people choose where they may wish to eat, or have one dining room with an area set aside closer to the door for the people who may need a little more help. Then they will feel part of the community and not someone to be shoved under the carpet.

One benefit of going into a rental community is that in most cases the incoming resident is not obligated to show any financial statement, and just a few wanted a bank statement or some proof of financial stability. We wondered if that had to do with the fact that a good 90% of the places we visited did not have a financial statement of their own an inquiring Senior could see. If you were to make one of the biggest moves of your life, wouldn't you want to be assured the place you were moving into was solvent? It wasn't even the fact that they refused to show a statement, it was the attitude that accompanied the refusal.

If you have chosen a rental community and are looking at more than a few, it is prudent to read the lease agreement carefully. Almost all the ones we saw were month to month, with very few having a year's lease. The deposits varied greatly. Some require security deposits, some unit deposits, while others are entrance fees. They range from one month's rent to a flat fee. Most are refundable, some are not; make sure you find out. Thirty days notice is the standard, but the difference here is that in some places if you give notice after the fifteenth, then the rest of the month is not pro-rated, whereas before the fifteenth it is. An interesting development in the business is a smoker's assessment in many of the communi-

ties. This is usually a flat fee up to $350 and is used to repaint and clean carpets and draperies when a smoker moves out. There's nothing worse than having that cigarette smell permeate everything you own when you don't even smoke. The last, but we think most crucial, question to address when looking at these communities is what is the increase per year in the monthly assessment. The range was anywhere from 2% to 11%, but the average seemed to be around 4%. If you are on a fixed income, you'll need to factor in this increase over a period of years to figure out how long you could live there on your income. Don't get caught! When we asked all these facilities if they told people of the increase or if it was spelled out in the contract, an astounding 70% said no.

Having a pet for some older adults is like having a child, so this can be a big consideration in choosing a community. Most places do allow pets. Some have an assessment for them similar to the smokers assessment, and some have rules that you must abide by if you do have a pet. For example, one place stipulated that the pet can not be over 10 pounds, so if you have a gorilla or a Pootsie that likes to eat, leave them at home. A word of caution—we were surprised one day when visiting a community when we saw everyone carrying their pets in the foyer. When asked why, they said there was a rule stating you must carry your pet from your apartment to the outside, so if you have a hard time walking yourself, you could have a little problem.

Downsizing is difficult enough, but moving to a community that only has studios in the assisted living section can be a real drag. You are forced to downsize twice. Half the places we visited had smaller units in assisted living and some even required you to share an apartment. If size is an issue for you, then please check this out carefully. Even if they do have larger units, find out how many, if there is a waiting list for those, and most importantly if they take people directly into assisted living, from the outside and by the way, most do. Be prepared to pay for the move from one level of care to another. When a single person needs additional care and must move, it's a pretty straight forward operation, however when a couple is involved, that's another matter. Both people would pay a monthly assessment separate from the other, which could run as high as $5,000 per month. If one of a couple needs additional care, in some cases the community makes both people move. If you're lucky you may get a small deduction in the well person's fee. You can see how important this question is, along with the annual increase in monthly assessment, in determining if you can afford a certain community. The cost difference from independent living to assisted living ranges anywhere from 25% to 60%. You should also know that the decision to move from one level of care to another is not determined by the resident as much as by a team of people at the community and, hopefully, the family. If you think Mom or Dad needs more help and they are not getting it, then by all means talk to the management. There does come a time when the community may not be appropriate any longer but they want Mom to stay because of the revenue from all the additional care. If a person is beginning to skip meals and wants room service, you can expect 7 to 10 free trays, then a cost of about $3.50 per tray from then on. This is to discourage people from staying in their rooms, when they should be out and about.

In the rental communities with a third level of care there are additional issues to be addressed. Is the facility certified for Medicare? Are residents guaranteed a place in the Skilled Nursing Facility? This is important to understand. A community, unless it is old and well established, can't afford to run a Skilled section without opening it up to the public. If a resident needs a bed and there is not one available, then that community will find a temporary place in another skilled facility and when the first bed becomes open, that resident will be moved back. This does not happen all the time, but it does happen, so be prepared for it. If a community says they guarantee you a spot in the skilled section, ask specifically what skilled section. If you do get the spot in the skilled, don't expect a private room, as most three level rental communities don't have private rooms in the nursing section, but you might luck out.

Food seems to loom the largest on the horizon as a major concern. The assigned seating rule seemed to be favored by the majority of communities, even if not by the residents. Find out about the meal plans. Are you required to pay for meals if you don't eat them and can you choose how many you would like per month?

Do you like your big meal in the middle of the day or are you the cosmopolitan type who likes to eat late? How about choices? Do you have grilled cheese everyday of your life or does a good Chinese Chicken Salad push your buttons? Don't get lazy when looking for your new home. If you have someone helping, be sure you stay in the loop. You're the one that will be living there so you should have the final say on which community you move to. And don't be snowed by all the amenities. It's more important to have a good and caring staff, than waiters in tuxedos serving in the dining room.

10.
Continuing Care and Lifecare Communities with No Equity

*T*he term "continuing care" covers a wide range of programs offered today. Most of the continuing care communities share the same physical features and usually have the same amenities as the Lifecare and buy-ins with equity. They are high-rises, cottages, townhouses, and apartment-type buildings, many with beautiful landscaping and some with flower and vegetable gardens where the residents work in the summer. Because there are so many variations in the contracts, it is extremely important to understand what you will be covered for in the event you need additional medical help.

There is a great deal of misunderstanding surrounding the Lifecare/Continuing Care contracts. Here's a simple definition. Lifecare means care forever on the same premises (excluding acute) with no increase except for the yearly inflation increases. Continuing Care means forever, but at additional costs as you need more care, and not necessarily on the same premises.

Lifecare is a form of continuing care, but it takes it one step further. It is usually referred to as the "extensive care plan." Through the years, however, the concept of these communities has changed. The differences between the two types of facilities is not as glaring as it was. People are living longer and moving into communities at a much older age, therefore they're not likely to be as healthy when

they move in. For this reason, Lifecare communities are now specifying certain illnesses that will exclude a person from medical
coverage for these conditions upon entering the community. This
means you may not be covered financially if you are diagnosed with
one of the excluded illnesses, or have a pre-existing condition.
Lifecare is, in many people's minds, a form of long term care insurance. You pay a little more to buy in than in a continuing care
community, but the financial security of knowing that once you are
in you won't have an increase in your medical costs as long as you
live, can be reassuring. In addition, if you die or develop a disease
or physical problem that can't be treated on site, you will be sent to
the appropriate facility and cared for at no additional cost. Lifecare
communities usually require you to use their doctors. However, you
can use your own, paying the Medicare or HMO deductible.

For couples, Lifecare can be the most cost effective program
out there. The reason is, that if one partner needs additional care,
there is never an increase in cost, even if you are both living in
different sections of the Lifecare community. You will want to find
out, however, if you can move to a smaller apartment upon the
death of a spouse, because the cost of your future medical needs is
based on the size of the apartment in which you live.

The terms "pay-as-you-go" and "a la carte" are a few definitions
for programs at continuing care communities. The proponents of
this type of care feel that if you buy in at a higher price (as in
Lifecare), you may be subsidizing other people if you never need the
additional medical services. They espouse the "pay-as-you-go" theo-
ry. These facilities also let you use your own doctor, but that is
because you are paying extra for the additional care you will receive.

And here is the rub. In one continuing care community we visited, you buy in, and as you need additional care you pay almost the market value for the additional services. Ask yourself, "Why should I spend the money to buy in, if it will cost me almost the same for the extra care if I was renting?" Even the long term care insurance policies provided as part of the monthly assessment don't cover assisted living, and will only cover the skilled nursing facility if you are there on a permanent basis.

A "non-equity" contract can be called a service contract, a continuum of care contract, an umbrella of care, care and residents agreement, and so on. The older Lifecare and Continuing Care communities were originally church-sponsored, taking care of their flock until the end. These places were there to care for their Seniors regardless of their illness or impairment. These communities are mostly non-profit and are well established, with ample financial resources. Some are also non-profit fraternal organizations. In these buildings, you do not own your own apartment. It is given back to the community upon your death. In the event you are not sure you will like the place you have chosen, you have a three month probation period in which to get your money back if you decide to move out, minus whatever costs the community incurred. If you stay, the total cost is amortized over a five year period, affording you time to change your mind, obviously getting back less each year. This is only if you decide to move. If you die before five years, your estate gets nothing back. In Lifecare and Continuing Care, medical assistance is readily available as your needs change and there is a life long assurance of service and health care.

Entrance fees for Continuing Care communities are generally lower than Lifecare, and range according to the geographic area, location, and amenities offered. The range for both can be anywhere from $18,000 to $600,000. You may be required to pay a deposit and a waiting list deposit, which may be applied to the entrance fee. Part of this entrance fee is deemed to be medical costs, so even though you can not use this buy-in against your capital gains tax, you can deduct it from your taxes as a medical expense. In the past, in order for Continuing Care communities to compete with the Lifecare programs, they came up with a refund system for your entrance fee. However, the Lifecare communities are now following the lead and are beginning to offer the same types of programs. Before you get too excited about this, pay attention. Most of the places we spoke with had devised a program which let you get back 25% to 50% of your entrance fee. This, however, is based on the fact that instead of paying the going rate for a one bedroom at $136,000, you would pay $190,000. You could only get this percentage back after a given period of time, in most cases 30 months. So you paid $54,000 for the opportunity to get a refund which would be $14,000. Here you must determine if you have enough available cash on hand to do this, and if you would be losing more in interest than the money you would be getting back. You must also pay taxes on the money you get back, which may have already been taxed. So if you see a refund offered, understand the conditions before committing yourself. There is also something called imputed interest. When a community is trying to get a permit to build, they are generally required to have as much as 50% to 60% of the apartments sold before they can begin building. The people who put the money down to hold a reservation are loaning the corporation the money. The IRS says that if you loan the money, then you must be getting interest, but in this case you are actually not getting interest. When you move in, you may be required to pay tax on the interest you did not, in fact, receive. Complicated? You bet. Again, check it out!

In some Lifecare communities there is still a maximum age limit, but it is slowly being raised as the age of the applicants gets older. In Continuing Care communities there isn't usually a maximum age, because you will be paying extra for the additional care you receive. To be accepted in the Independent Living section you must be ambulatory. You will need to fill out medical forms, and in some cases go before an admissions review committee to see if you have all your marbles. Just plan on having a thorough medical evaluation. Continuing Care and Lifecare communities are like most others in that they take people directly into the Skilled Nursing Facility. They buy in at a small fee and are accepted as private pay patients. Many of these communities have started taking people directly into the assisted living sections. If a resident of a facility needs to be moved to a higher level and there is no room, the community will find him or her a place in another facility, and pay the difference if there is any, until a space opens up in the community. The resident obviously gets priority when a bed does become available. Mr. Sterling did not understand this policy because he assumed the phrase "we will take care of you on site for the rest of your life" meant just that. When his wife became ill and required time in the Skilled Nursing Facility, there was not a bed available and she was sent to another facility. He raised such a stink, they changed the ad and the policy.

In these communities, the financial requirements can be a little different from others. Financial statements are usually mandatory, as well as tax returns and sometimes joint tenancy agreements. You are required to have a minimum amount of money in your account and the money must be in your name. You will probably have to have Medicare. It's a good idea to check into the Medicare question as some of the communities are not Medicare approved, presenting the possibility of extra costs in the event of an illness.

When looking for the first time, be aware that most Continuing Care communities do not allow private pay caregivers in your own unit, but Lifecare does. This means that in Continuing Care communities if you reach a point where you may need more help, you have to move. Wheelchairs and walkers are allowed, however some communities still prohibit them in the dining room. Many of the assisted living apartments are smaller than those in Independent living. If there is a separate dining room in assisted living, find out if you are free to go from one to the other. In Continuing Care, the additional cost in monthly assessment to move from one level to another can be a considerable amount. From Independent Living to Assisted Living it can range from 30% to 100%, and from Assisted Living to the Skilled Nursing Facility it can be from 25% to 50%. A couple living apart from each other may have to pay two monthly assessments. Also, in Continuing Care, there can be a limit to the size apartment a single person can have. If you're a single gal with a four closet wardrobe, this might not work for you. Most facilities do not provide for acute care, do not cover medications, psychological problems, alcohol related problems, drug treatment, dental, and eye problems. Unless an Alzheimer's unit has been built or a program is available, the community can not care for these patients as the illness progresses.

Long term care insurance policies are offered in many of the Continuing Care communities. If they are offered, it is only to those who qualify upon entrance, and again, in most communities, it does not cover Assisted Living, and only kicks in if you are permanently in the Skilled Nursing Facility. In most cases the policy covers about one third to one half of the cost of the Skilled Nursing Facility. The monthly costs vary according to the community and the coverage offered. Some of the exclusions in coverage are Lou Gehrig's disease, Alzheimer's, rheumatoid arthritis, MS, chronic bronchitis, and kidney disorders. Many of these same illnesses are excluded in Lifecare if you are diagnosed before moving in. It's important to understand that even though a Continuing Care community advertises a continuum of care, if you do not qualify for the insurance program you will be paying almost the market rate for any additional care you receive.

Food is important to everyone and is a bright spot in the day of most Seniors. Find out about the meal plans, if you are required to take every meal, the variety of choices offered, whether there is assigned seating, and if there is a private dining room for you to throw a bash if you are a party animal, or if you can have a tray in your room for Monday Night Football. You might also want to ask how many sick trays you get before you start being charged. The annual monthly assessment increase per year averages between 2% and about 5% and is not always stated in the contract. Ask to see a financial statement if you're curious where the money goes. In most of the non-profit communities they have one to show. Family members are not encouraged to stay in the residents' apartments, so if a son who can't find a job wants to move in, you're the one that's in luck. Check to see if there are any additional charges for a parking space, does the hairdresser do every resident's hair the same way, and do they throw fun parties with a little stick in the punch from time to time. Also the pet situation can be an issue here, as many of these places do not allow dogs and cats. Ask who decides when a person needs to move to another level of care and remember, if you

get a call saying your favorite sunny apartment is available and you turn it down, you may end up at the end of the line again.

All these communities have something to offer, some more than others, and as individual needs vary so do Continuing Care and Lifecare communities. Dressing up for dinner may be what you're used to, while someone else wants to wear the housecoat that can pass for a dress in a pinch. Visit, read the brochures, ask a million questions, and talk to the residents. Your intuition usually guides you in the right direction, if your pocketbook doesn't.

11.
Continuing Care Communities With Equity

Lifecare communities are changing. The traditional Lifecare community described in the previous chapter has evolved in some areas of the country. There are now communities which offer continuing benefits of lifecare combined with the advantages of ownership. In these communities, you either buy as a condominium or you purchase shares in a cooperative according to square footage, which entitles you to all the benefits of home ownership. You basically own your own unit, and if you move out or die there are no monthly fees to the estate. You may list it for sale with the community or any realtor. There is a transfer fee which goes to the community. Again, be sure to check these new types of communities thoroughly. You or someone you trust must understand the intricacies of the disposal of the unit and the costs involved before deciding to move. With more people moving to retirement communities in the last ten years, it was clear that Seniors needed to be given more choices in their living arrangements. The concept of buy-ins with equity began to take shape. Many large hotel chains, such as Marriott, corporations, and even families jumped on the bandwagon and senior management firms sprang up to manage these communities.

The difference in a buy-in with equity versus other types of communities is that you actually own your own apartment and, in many instances, you own part of the common areas as well. They range from offering no care at all to Continuing Care and some even offer Lifecare. They come in many varieties, with each offering something different, and at prices across the board. In most cases, you can't be faint of heart when inquiring about the price of these apartments. These communities cater to about 1% of the Senior population, so you can imagine how expensive they can be. The average Senior probably could not afford them. Some fall under the auspices of the Department of Social Services, while others under the Department of Real Estate, therefore they are governed by different laws, thus having an effect on how the communities are run.

We were surprised by the difference in the sizes of apartments and in the costs for same size units. When these communities were first built, many developers didn't think it through and included too many studios in the configuration of the building. After finding they were the most difficult to sell, they began combining them. There are still places that have studios, but in general the one-bedroom seems to be the biggest seller. Many do not have full kitchens which is hard to understand, so before buying, find out if you can put one in. Some of the fancier places offer a two bedroom, two bath with den and fireplace, so basically you can get whatever you want.

Seniors have opted for the buy-ins with equity for many reasons; they like the idea of owning something, they have a capital gains problem they don't want to deal with (let the kids figure it out), they think they are throwing their money away if they move into a community that has no equity, and they don't want to rent. They can also do whatever they want to the apartment because they own it, even to the extent of tearing out bathrooms or kitchens. Yet, even owning your own unit doesn't give you carte blanche, there are still rules. One of the rules we heard that had us in stitches was, "If you have a pet that qualifies in size and weight, bring it on in. However, if that pet dies you can not replace it with another." So our advice to you is get a puppy if you plan to move.

Again we found there is no uniformity in the names these communities go by. They call themselves a Lifecare with Equity, a Care Community with Equity, and a Congregate Care Independent Living Community with Services. These buy-ins range from one level of care to three levels, while many have an Alzheimer's wing as the fourth level. The most common seems to be two levels with an affiliation with an independent Skilled Nursing Facility. If this is the type of community you are thinking about, make sure the Skilled Nursing Facility that is part of the medical plan is one in which you would want to live. If not, double check on the long term care insurance that is offered by these communities. If you qualify, make sure you will be covered if you have to go to a different Skilled Nursing Facility. This is very important. The future of these communities is having all the levels of care on the same premises. It's a move in the right direction.

The financial aspects of these communities can be very hard to understand for anyone, and in some cases it can be downright misleading. The rules are complicated and they need to be studied carefully before any commitment is made. The entrance fee is obviously the first to consider. As with any business, the range of prices for any given object can vary tremendously. The fee is generally based on the area of the country, the size of the unit and the amenities included, the location of the community, and the competition. You can pay as little as $15,000 and as much as $1.5 million, believe it or not. Aside from the purchase price, many places charge an additional entrance fee and a deposit to be on the reservation or waiting list. For those that do charge this, ask why. Is it refundable, or is it applied to the entrance fee or the first months' rent? People who are on a reservation list for a certain unit should consider the move when the unit becomes available. Most of the larger units are the preferred ones, so therefore they are not available as often. Too many times people continue to turn down a great apartment, only to find six months later that they really need to move and are forced to move into a not-so-desirable unit, or in the worse cases, they no longer qualify medically. This happens all the time. Mrs. Crandall had her name on a waiting list at Bunyon's Acres for two years and could never quite get off the dime. When she finally decided to move, her favorite unit had been sold since the community could not continue to hold its prime units. She signed up, passed the physical to be eligible for the Long Term Care Insurance, and was on her way. Before she actually bought the apartment, an old injury she had forgotten about but one that doctors told her would be a problem in the future resurfaced. She ended up in the hospital. Eventually, she was allowed to move in, but without the Long Term Care Insurance. This meant a much heavier financial burden to her if she needed any additional medical care in the future and she hadn't been lucky enough to hit a lottery.

Because many of these places are very costly, it's no wonder there are financial requirements for moving in. Most demand a financial statement, some require a minimum annual income, others an income two and one half times the monthly assessment, or a flat monthly income. We had to laugh when we discovered a few communities whose entrance requirements were stiffer than the most prestigious country club in town. So expect to supply personal references and wear that St. John's knit when you go to your first screening.

The physical requirements can be as stringent as the social or financial ones. There are many assessments needed to get the nod. You may be visited in your home by the community's nurse. And going before the admissions committee can be as tough as taking an oral exam. One clue we offer is if you go with your parents to look at a community, let them do most of the talking. People are suspect if the kids don't shut up, and answer for Mom and Dad every time a question is asked.

An important issue to inquire about when looking into buy-ins with equity, is whether or not they take outsiders directly into the on-site skilled nursing section. If they do, you need to know if they will find a place for you if they are full, and if you have priority for moving back in. If you are ill, find out if trays are delivered to the rooms at mealtimes, for how long and at what cost, if any. Some newer communities even have room service, but most likely it's at an additional charge. There again is no set rule as to the number of meals offered with the purchase price. The majority offered only one meal with the purchase price, but all had full dining room service with considerable choices at mealtimes. Some offer a certain number per month. Check to see if you get a credit if they are not used, and if someone other than you can use them. If you have a caregiver, ask if she is allowed to eat in the dining room, must she wear a uniform, and must she pay the full price for her meals.

Owning your own apartment gives you options that other types of buy-ins do not. If you are ambulatory or can transfer by yourself from a wheelchair, you may have your own caregiver in your independent unit. Wheelchairs and walkers are allowed everywhere. In many places they do have assisted living sections, but you are not required to move there unless you become unable to manage with a caregiver in the independent section. Ask if you are relegated to the assisted living section if you can go into the independent areas. For couples, it can get expensive if each is living in a different section. Usually the apartments in the assisted living wing are smaller than in the independent section. Ask about the increase in the monthly assessment if you must move to another level, and also how much more you might pay as a couple if you are separated. Inquire what happens to your unit if you must move. This is an area where costs can escalate, so you must know precisely how this works in the different communities, making sure it is spelled out to your satisfaction in the contract. In the majority of the communities you can't rent your apartment. If you are paying additional monies in another level, you will still be required to pay a non-use assessment after a certain length of time, which can be as high as 85% of the original monthly assessment.

When the time comes to sell your unit, it is important to know what restrictions and rules apply. The differences in the procedures can amount to a considerable bit of money. Many people say that buying a unit in a retirement community is not a particularly sound investment unless you live there for at least six years. You need time for your unit to appreciate to offset the costs when you sell, or if the community is new, to give the marketing department time to sell all the original units, thereby making your apartment more valuable and desirable. It's hard to imagine the marketing people pushing units that have already sold before ones that have never sold. It's just common sense. Also, the commission when selling a unit is higher with a new apartment than one that has already been sold. Find out if you can use your own agent. Mr. Merriweather had been a broker and his two sons were agents. When he needed to sell his unit, he was surprised to learn only the community agent could sell it. Think he was upset? You bet, but mainly at himself for assuming he could sell it. Most communities take a percentage of the appreciation ranging from 50% to 75%. On top of that, most charge a transfer fee of between 7% and 10% based on the selling price. If you can use an outside agent, be clear that you then must pay them an additional 3% to 6% depending on how the sale is handled. This can add up to quite a bit of money. Also ask who determines the selling price and if you can sell to whomever you want. In most places you can, but obviously they must meet the community's standards.

Subsidizing residents in a buy-in with equity is not something you usually see. A few places said they put part of the transfer fee into a special account just for that purpose. Most said they let the person stay, putting a lien on their apartment. When the resident dies, the community deducts what is owed them with interest from the sale. A reverse mortgage may also be an answer to a cash flow problem. In the past, most communities made you pay all cash for your apartment, having no mortgage. Now the times are changing. You may be able to get in with a down-payment. You will then have a monthly mortgage payment, as well as the monthly assessment. This can put a dent in the old pocketbook. Ask what the yearly increase in the monthly assessment is; sometimes they neglect to mention it or it isn't in the contract so it slips through the cracks. This can cause havoc with your finances a few years down the road. It was interesting that 75% of the places we visited did not have a financial statement for the prospective resident to see. Most were for profit and out of the non-profits only one was using the Charitable Remainder Trust.

Obviously, medical services are at the top of the list when checking out these communities. Are they "a la carte" and do they even have them on site? A major component of the medical services is the long term care insurance package, which is becoming quite popular but which you must understand completely before signing on the dotted line. When you read the advertisements for this type of community, most say you will be taken care of for life with their extensive medical plan. The reality is, many prospective residents, because they are waiting too long to move in, do not qualify for the plan. This isn't necessarily because of age but because of other physical problems, some of which include Alzheimer's, Parkinson's, hypertension, diabetes, heart problems, cancer, stroke, emphysema and their pre-existing conditions. Part of your monthly assessment is the cost of the long term care insurance and it varies according to the extent of the plan. This is really the meat of the program. The policies range from:

- Coverage for life to a limited amount of time.

- Payment for all medical needs while in a Skilled Nursing Facility or having home care.

- Room and board, but all supplies extra.

- 80% of the cost of the care to a much smaller percentage.

- Very rarely complete coverage.

- Limitations on where you can be treated.

- Mandatory acceptance of the coverage if you qualify, even if you have your own long term care insurance.

Don't make the mistake Mrs. Lazar did. Not fully understanding the policy and thinking she was completely covered, she was shocked when she had to go the Skilled Nursing Facility and was covered only for $90 a day when the room actually cost $175. To add insult to injury, she had to pay for all the extras, including her own Kleenex. Also, some don't kick in until you've had a stay in the hospital. Check this out. These policies change on a daily basis and usually to the detriment of the Senior.

We want you to be so aware of the pitfalls in some contracts and what you may be getting in for so that you can plan accordingly. It's one thing to be told all the details and make a conscious decision. But to be surprised in a moment of crisis is another thing. Read the fine print, have someone else read the contract too, don't be embarrassed to ask a million questions, and when you go for lunch or dinner, ask to be seated with one of the residents, not the marketing director. If you don't ask, you might not be told. It's worth it. Living in a community such as this can be a wonderful experience if you understand what it's all about.

Diana and Phil were pioneers in the field, or so they thought when they purchased their long term care insurance. Even though they were both in their early seventies and healthy, they decided to go ahead and spring for the $4,000 per year on a premium policy. Five years down the line, they decided to move to Spring Gardens. They were so excited to share with the staff the fact that they were 80% covered for all their long term medical needs. Guess what the bad news was? They were required to take the community's insurance plan because they qualified, and had to pay an additional $600 per month for coverage that was less than what they already had. Because people are buying these insurance policies more often now, you need to find out the rules of the place you're interested in. In the future, we're sure the policies will be much more lenient and the prospective resident will have a choice.

Because people are buying their units, there is usually no age limit. When these communities, most of them not more than five to ten years-old, were built, they marketed themselves to the "active Senior." Now, as the years have passed, this is slowly becoming a problem, as the once active Senior who moved in six years ago may now be frail. Postponing the move, or the inability to make a decision, can be problematic because even though you are buying, there are still health requirements to be met, and if they offer long term care insurance as part of their program you probably wouldn't qualify. The other problem for the community is the age-old question of how infirm a person must be before he's turned down. The community has a responsibility to respect the wishes of the existing residents.

12.
Assisted Living Facilities

Assisted Living facilities are appropriate for individuals who are unable to function in an independent living environment, but who don't require the level of supervision and care of a nursing facility. While these establishments go by a variety of names, depending on local jurisdiction's definition, we're talking about a rental or buy-in complex of rooms and apartments, or cottages, where residents are provided with nurses and other health care professionals on staff or available on-call should a need arise. Meals are included—often there's a main dining room, a snack shop, a salad bar, and a coffee shop. There are usually a broad range of activities designed to stimulate social contact, and staff members whose purpose is to promote a somewhat active lifestyle within the community. Many facilities are affiliated with or located near medical resources, or private-pay help can assist a resident.

Most states have guidelines covering these facilities, and a Resident Assessment for personalized care is one of the first items for consideration. If you or your parents are planning to move to an Assisted Living facility, you'll have to have a complete physical examination and then have the facility's staff evaluate your physical and mental status. Most residents need assistance with Activities of Daily Living (ADLs) some of which include bathing, dressing, grooming, eating, housekeeping and medication monitoring, and the staff oversees these things.

When is Assisted Living no longer a viable option? Managers reported they find their facilities unsuitable for those who wander, whose incontinence affects other residents, cannot feed themselves, are bedridden, are incapable of transferring in and out of bed, and who require skilled care services such as oxygen administration, colostomy apparatus and breathing machines.

The monthly rental plan usually requires one month's rent deposit, with about a 3% rent increase per year. Everything is included; all utilities, housekeeping and linen service, and usually you can bring your own furniture. About the only extras are cable service, the telephone bill, your beauty shop and drugstore charges, and perhaps a smoker's assessment if you haven't kicked the habit. The trips and entertainment are free, and in some places you can take a small pet. Basic monthly rents vary in this type of community, depending on the part of the country, the age and condition of the buildings, and how many extras they offer. Costs vary; in some places you'll find subsidies, and in others you can expect all private pay residents. Our survey showed a range from $846 for a subsidized shared room in rural Maryland with minimal assistance, to $4,065 for a one bedroom apartment in urban California where the resident needed help with just about everything. There are a lot of Alzheimer's patients in Assisted Living facilities, and many have a special wing for more advanced cases. Check to see what's around an Assisted Living facility, how easy is it going to be to get Dad to his doctor appointments or do they have physicians on call?

Other questions to ask:

▌ How often are residents assessed, and how do you inform the family of any changes in status?

▌ What's the annual rent increase?

▌ Are there banking services on site?

▌ Is there transportation provided to church?

▌ Can I hire a companion, and if so, can she/he live with me? What are the rates?

▌ Can a companion go into the dining room with me?

▌ What are the rules governing companions? Ask for a copy.

▌ Is there assigned seating in the dining room?

▌ How often can I have a sick tray delivered to my room, and what are the charges?

▌ Is it possible to have guests for holiday meals?

■ Is there a dress code for the dining room? Madge loved her slippers and moved to another Assisted Living facility when she was barred from the dining room for showing up in her furry pink favorites.

■ Is there a pharmacy that will deliver?

■ Do you have pull cords in apartments in case of emergency?

■ Do you hold scheduled fire drills?

■ Is there a little garden space I could use?

■ If I move from one apartment to another for personal reasons, is there a charge?

■ Is your laundry done for you and is there a charge?

■ What are the additional Assisted Living Service charges?

■ Should I carry my own insurance for the contents of my apartment?

■ What's the policy on smoking?

■ Can wheelchairs go into all areas?

■ Is there anywhere in my apartment to lock valuables?

■ Is there a security system that alerts staff that you've left your room?

13.
Choosing a Skilled Nursing Facility

S killed nursing facility, nursing center, convalescent hospital, nursing home or nursing care facility—what are these and why are there so many different names? As the health care industry changes in our country, so do facilities, services and group plans. Health Care Centers now provide personal care, assisted care and complete intermediate and skilled nursing care, and you had better take a stab at understanding what's out there before your parents need one. A nursing care facility, or nursing home, basically provides care to those who need nursing care but who don't need to be hospitalized. This care may be needed after major surgery, an accident or after leaving a hospital. Perhaps you need rehabilitation care, such as daily physical therapy for a broken hip, or daily speech therapy after a stroke, and you're too frail to go home. An essential element to grasp regarding nursing facilities is that levels of care vary even within the same facility, ranging from intensive round-the-clock nursing care for the seriously sick, to personal care with minimal assistance without any active nursing or other medical care. Whatever the place chooses to call itself, investigate the care provided and check in advance with both the facility and with Medicare, Medicaid and your private insurance carrier to see what's covered. Be sure to check if the facility you choose accepts Medicaid in case your funds run out. That way your parents won't have to move more than once. Before choosing a facility, you might want to contact the Long Term Care Ombudsman Inc. This group promotes the highest quality of life and care for residents of nursing facilities, and can help families and staff with inquiries and complaints. Tell the Ombudsman which facilities you are considering and ask for information about any complaints that have been lodged against them, and how those complaints were resolved. They aren't a referral agency, so don't count on them recommending one place over another. You should discuss the complaints when interviewing the staff to find out exactly what has been done to prevent recurrence. Be persistent about getting your questions answered, and don't accept any passing of the buck, as this level of care for the elderly is fraught with violations, inconsistencies in legislation, and fraud. Nearly all people entering a nursing facility have had the decision of where to go made by someone else.

Hospital-based skilled nursing facilities, also called extended care facilities, are departments within hospitals. They provide the highest levels of nursing care, and are intended to be next in the hierarchy after acute hospital care. These aren't meant for long term residence, as they're very expensive, (starting around $200 a day) and the average stay is usually for a few weeks. A non-hospital-based skilled nursing facility is suitable for someone requiring comprehensive, intensive nursing care and 24-hour supervision. It can be called a convalescent hospital standing alone, be part of a health care center, or be a wing in a continuing care retirement community. Skilled Nursing facilities are licensed to provide a multitude of services including tube feeding, tracheostomy care, respiratory and intravenous therapy, Alzheimer's Care and respite care. A Skilled Nursing facility can be for either short-term, post-hospitalization

recovery, or long-term for permanent impairment, serious chronic illness, or just being old and frail. Just about the only thing you can't get in a Skilled Nursing facility is acute care, meaning no surgery and no ventilators. Medicare and private insurance will pay only up to their coverage limits, and only if care has been prescribed specifically by a physician and the patient has been discharged from an acute care hospital. A Skilled Nursing facility can be part of a comprehensive health care center, meaning that as you require less care and supervision you can move down to the next level, which is an Intermediate Nursing Care facility.

This level of care is suitable for those who are unable to live independently, but who don't require intensive care. These places provide medical attention and assistance with eating, dressing and bathing, and there's always a licensed vocational or practical nurse on duty. Generally, only basic physical therapy is included in the cost, although other rehabilitative therapies can be arranged for extra fees. Don't count on Medicare coverage in Intermediate Care facilities, but you might find a private policy that will offer coverage. Usually Intermediate Care facilities don't stand alone because they can't charge as much as Skilled Nursing facilities, and also because they don't get Medicare patients.

Be wary of multi-level facilities that are so diversified that the personalized attention so important to a long term resident can suffer. A typical case in point is Marge, who broke both her hips falling on a slippery deck while on a cruise in the Baltic. She endured weeks in a hospital's acute care facility, then moved into a Skilled Nursing facility, then to an Intermediate Care facility where she languished for nearly a year. Her daughter was visiting an aunt, who was happily ensconced in an Assisted Living community, enjoying a quality of life she thought wasn't possible. Marge's daughter realized her mother was practically a vegetable back at the multilevel facility, with very little stimulation, no outings, and a grim outlook. Once Marge had Mom transferred to Sylvan Fields, where she received loving care and companionship, everybody's spirits were lifted. Again, always pay careful attention to the payment requirements of any facility. Initial Medicare or private insurance coverage for a Skilled Nursing facility doesn't mean coverage will continue after Mom switches to a non-skilled level.

The only way to determine if a nursing home is a good one is to visit it yourself—several times if possible. Speak to the staff and residents, and keep your eyes open. Get to know the administrators, and go at night when the staff is different and check out the atmosphere. As there are virtually no objective guidelines when sudden illness or other circumstances might force you to move a relative to a nursing home, you'll have to wing it. And while the state or county Ombudsman will hear a lot of complaints about facilities, many are unwilling to badmouth them. Your best bet in uncovering blatant violations is to read the state inspection report, also known as the state survey, administered by a government agency called the Health Care Financing Administration. This group, HCFA, certifies over 16,000 nursing homes that receive monies from Medicare or Medicaid. While these reports spell out how a facility treats its residents and evaluate everything from safety hazards, use of restraints, and medication errors, to the quality of life, they're not always readily available. Nursing homes with loads of violations and deficiencies love to lose or hide them, or give you an outdated copy. Many places say it's simply not available, so you'll have to trust your instincts and your nose. If an administrator won't show you a copy, forget it, assume they're hiding something, and move on to the next place on your list. Try asking your family physician; doctors know who has a good reputation. And, if you do read the inspection report, be sure you personally go there unannounced to see if it is all true. If Medicaid coverage is what you're looking for, make sure the facility meets the requirements. In addition, you should check:

▌ Is the location suitable for the patient—convenient for family and friends to visit?

▌ Are the interior and grounds well maintained—go around

to the back, and see how the garbage area checks out. If that area is immaculate, you'll have an idea as to other areas not intended for viewing.

- Observe and talk with residents—do they seem well cared for, clean shaven and comfortable, dressed appropriately?

- Are residents up and moving? Are those in wheelchairs moved frequently? Do they stare at the walls or TV?

- Are residents talking among themselves? Involved in activities?

- Do all the bedrooms open onto a corridor and have windows, as required by law?

- Is the staff caring or do they appear to be overworked and harried? This is a bad sign and might mean the residents aren't receiving adequate care.

- Are there adequate wheelchair ramps and wide hallways so two wheelchairs can pass easily?

- Dining and activity rooms—Is there adequate staff for the residents?

- Are exits marked clearly? Do you see a sprinkler system and fire extinguishers? Are patient areas well lighted? Are fire, evacuation and disaster plans posted? We opened what we assumed was a closet door in a nursing home and found four startled employees enjoying a break, smoking, tugging on a residents' leftover lemonade, and gossiping up a storm.

▎ Are there no-smoking areas, and is it enforced? Are there press-down door handles rather than knobs?

▎ Take a big whiff, and if the place has a bad odor, forget it. Strong chemical products shouldn't be covering up smells, and conscientious care isn't being provided if unpleasant odors are being masked. What's more, it's unhealthy for patients to breathe these fumes all day.

▎ Make sure there's a physician available for emergencies.

▎ Are residents' rooms bright and cheerful, well-ventilated, fitted with individual thermostats?

▎ Are bathing and toilet areas private? Grab bars on toilets and bathtubs?

▎ Is fresh drinking water within easy reach of the bed, and is the pitcher clean?

▎ Are residents allowed to decorate their rooms? Hang pictures?

■ Is there counter space for personal items? Is there a private phone?

■ Does the staff show respect to the residents? Is the staff friendly toward you? Are employees dressed neatly? Do the residents seem at ease with staff?

■ Do the residents seem appropriate for the setting? Think twice about a place that permits Alzheimer's patients to disrupt the routines of others.

■ Are Patients Rights posted? Enforced? Do patients know what their rights are?

■ Do residents appear to like the food? Do you like the looks of the food? Does the staff feed residents who cannot feed themselves? Will the home provide special diets such as low cholesterol or low salt? Are tables easily accessible to wheelchairs?

■ Can residents eat in their rooms if they prefer? Can a visitor share a meal in the dining room with a resident?

■ Can snacks be brought into the facility?

■ Are snacks and juices provided during the day?

■ Does the facility have arrangements with a nearby hospital to transfer residents in an emergency?

■ Does the facility have an arrangement with a nearby pharmacy to deliver medications?

▌ Look around at the residents—are most of them in restraints? This could mean the home can't keep people safe, or the staff isn't bothering to work with the patients. And look for bedsores—this is a giveaway that neglect is bigtime. Or it's grossly understaffed.

▌ Can you continue to use your current pharmacy?

▌ How are drugs dispensed? Do they use the unit method?

▌ Is a social worker on staff? Is it possible to attend religious services?

▌ Is Grandmother sitting in dirty clothes or is personal laundry done regularly?

▌ Are there special events and holiday parties for residents?

The American Healthcare Association, a nonprofit federation of state associations that represents more than 11,000 long term care facilities nationwide, recommends that you inquire about quality assurance programs. Ask if the home you are considering participates in the Long Term Care Accreditation Program of the Joint Commission on Accreditation of Healthcare Organizations, which surveys nursing homes to make sure they meet certain standards. Remember, a beautiful facility can be a facade; the goal is to get past the appearance of the building and the phony smile of the administrator, and look at the relationships between staff and residents. Every resident should be treated with dignity and the home should attempt to give residents the best quality of life possible. For a free guide to choosing a nursing home, send a self addressed stamped envelope to: "Thinking About A Nursing Home," American Health Care Association, 1201 L Street NW, Washington, DC 20005.

14.
Alzheimer's Facilities

Alzheimer's disease (AD) is a progressive, degenerative disease that attacks the brain and results in impaired memory, thinking and behavior, and it's estimated that by the year 2000, one in 100 Americans will have Alzheimer's. Why do we hear about so many cases, when twenty years ago very few families were affected by this killer? It's not a new disease—it was just as prevalent three generations ago, but our grandparents referred to it as hardening of the arteries or senility, and they mistakenly thought it was a normal part of aging. AD sneaks up on a family and can throw them into confusion, panic, anger and exhaustion. Problems remembering recent events and difficulty performing familiar tasks are early symptoms, and the patient may experience confusion, behavior and personality changes, as well as difficulty finding words, following directions, finishing thoughts and expressing himself. Disorientation in place and time, and problems with abstract thinking, are other symptoms which cause problems in everyday activities, and they may be recognizable in the following ways: frequently getting lost in familiar surroundings, forgetting appointments or errands, not recalling names of familiar people, or remembering who they are, frustration at not being able to handle money, and not being able to use the tools of daily living such as keys, or the telephone. How rapidly these changes occur will vary from person to person,

and not all patients exhibit all symptoms, but the disease eventually leaves its victims totally unable to care for themselves.

While there's no simple diagnostic test for Alzheimer's disease, a complete medical and neurological evaluation is strongly recommended when dementia symptoms are noticed. If your parents' physician can't suggest a qualified doctor to make the assessment, telephone the Alzheimer's Association Hotline at 1-800-621-0379, and request a local referral. Because of the seriousness of the disease, a second opinion is appropriate if there are any doubts about the diagnosis. Bev's neighbor ran a fantastic Alzheimer's Day Care facility, and she tried to suggest that Bev have her Dad checked out, as he was starting to lose it. While Bev had become increasingly worried about her Dad's mental deterioration, she couldn't face the fact that maybe he was a victim, so she continued to cover up his failings, hoping no one would notice and he'd get better. When it was finally diagnosed after he took the wrong freeway exit and was robbed by gang members, the Alzheimer's Day Care had a waiting list a mile long, and Bev had to quit her job to be his caregiver.

A complete evaluation should include:

■ A detailed medical history.

■ A thorough physical and neurological examination to rule out other disorders.

■ A mental status test essential to evaluate orientation, attention, recent recall, and the ability to calculate, read, write, name, copy drawings, repeat, understand and make judgments.

■ A psychiatric assessment to rule out other disorders.

■ Neuropsychological testing to measure a variety of functions including attention orientation, language skills and perception.

■ Routine laboratory tests, including blood work, a CT scan and an EKG.

This last category of tests is used to exclude such causes of dementia as vitamin deficiency, thyroid disease, chronic infections such as brain tumors, circulatory disease and multi-facet dementia (little strokes which are quite common). While none of these tests alone can make an Alzheimer's diagnosis, they're useful when their findings are considered together, and they can be used to identify or eliminate other potential causes of dementia. The only way to confirm a diagnosis of AD is to examine brain tissue under a microscope such as at autopsy, but professionals can spot the disease with amazing accuracy. Because of the seriousness of the disease, a second opinion

is appropriate if there are any doubts about the diagnosis.

Alzheimer's sufferers wear many hats, and a seasoned caregiver in a large Day Care Center summed it up this way, "It's like a supermarket of behaviors—you see gentle folks turn into combative Attilas; kind, caring people becoming frustrated and angry, with their inhibitions released from cages, and the worst part is the helplessness the family feels."

Nobody is regulating the care and treatment of this disease in our country. In other words, anybody can buy or rent a building in most places and rent rooms to people—it happens all the time. What occurs in a skilled nursing facility is a different matter, but as for parking elderly, frail confused people who don't require medical assistance it's wide open, much to the dismay of consumer advocates. But when there's a need in this country, chances are that somebody'll fill it, and there are some wonderful facilities in operation catering to Alzheimer's and dementia patients. As the disease is getting more attention, specialists have teamed up with developers and the result is excellent care in pleasant, appropriate surroundings.

Small Board and Care facilities across the country are full of Alzheimer's patients, many spending years staring at non-stop television, with no stimulation and very little attention, and all these operators need in many states to stay open is a permit to take renters. On the other hand, in many settings catering to Alzheimer's victims, people with dementia are taken on outings, encouraged to pursue their hobbies and interests, such as art and music, and enjoy a level of social activity appropriate for their level of disability.

How do you approach the variable needs of the parent with dementia? After the assessment, figure out what route seems best for all, bearing in mind that this is a progressive disease. Join a support group and pay attention to where other members have found success. This is an area where new places are springing up constantly.

You'll find freestanding Alzheimer's facilities incorporated into Assisted Living communities, and as special sections of Continuing Care and Lifecare communities. One of the most common settings is to have Alzheimer's patients housed in a wing of a nursing home devoted to patients with dementia. While there's no model of care for these facilities, you should have a good feeling about the place. Drop in unannounced and observe the following:

▌ What is their philosophy of care?

▌ Who are the residents?

▌ Does the setting provide a safe, secure and appropriate environment?

▌ Is there adequate supervision?

▌ Are the services designed to support the patients? For example, if you see several patients wandering or pacing, is there adequate room?

▌ Are considerations given to residents' privacy?

▌ Does the staff seem to reach out in a caring way, or do they leave the patients alone a lot?

▌ Do the residents appear to be bathed and well-groomed?

▌ What sort of a security system is in place? Is it relatively easy for you to leave?

If you're considering a rental in a residential setting for a parent with Alzheimer's, check out the following:

▌ Is there more than one level of care?

▌ What are the extra costs as the level of care escalates within the Alzheimer's setting?

▌ What is the entry deposit?, and is this refundable?

∎ What are the sizes of the rooms?

∎ What is the total cost per month?

∎ What is the ratio of staff to residents?

∎ Does the fee go up every year?

∎ Is there an occupational physical therapist on site?

∎ What is the meal and snack schedule?

∎ What special training does your staff have?

∎ What are the qualifications of your staff?

∎ What licenses do they have?

∎ Does Medicare cover any of the cost?

∎ What subsidies d'o you have?

∎ What care do you *not* provide?

■ Can residents use their own furniture?

■ What's your policy on physical restraints?

■ Are there appropriate activities and outings?

■ How often are patients assessed, and who does this?

■ Depending on your personal views, you might want to inquire about the Do Not Resuscitate policy.

■ At what point in my father's disease is your facility no longer appropriate? In other words, when is it time to move Dad?

15.
Low Income and Subsidized Housing

U nlike other housing alternatives for retirees, subsidized housing is usually characterized by long waiting lists for few vacancies, stringent income or lifestyle guidelines for applicants, and few options. We tend to think of subsidized housing as poorly constructed projects with few tenant amenities, surrounded by inner city blight. While this isn't always the case, you'll have to do some research to find the award winners. If you are the Senior, or know of one looking for some financial assistance with housing, it bears looking into all the alternatives. An older person hoping to find subsidized lodging in a large urban area might be told there's not much available now, particularly in a safe neighborhood, but they'll put you on a waiting list and in a couple of years something might open up. It's all supply and demand, but in some parts of this country Senior subsidized housing is available simply for the asking.

Let's look at government subsidized housing, whether it's federal, state, county, township or a combination of these. Many variables go into the equation of housing for the elderly, and a lot of it depends on where you live in the country, what your assets are, and the state of your health. If you are receiving SSI (Supplemental Security Income) which pays monthly checks to people who are 65 or older, or disabled or blind and who don't own much or have much income, you may be able to get other help from the state or county, in addition to Social Security, to help with housing costs. Many retirement residences have a few spaces reserved for SSI recipients at a flat rate which is less than the cost of the least expensive room.

If you're not flush with money, you might have to try a little creativity for your golden years. Take Ethel, a Los Angeles widow whose income and Social Security didn't cover the rent in a place she considered up to par. A friend at her church told her that his brother was living in a comfortable subsidized Seniors Only complex in Bisbe, Arizona, and that there were seven vacancies in the place. Ethel's pastor mentioned this to an elderly couple in his flock, and the next thing he knew he was driving the threesome plus another widower to Bisbe. The three who moved report that it took a bit to adjust, and they miss their friends, but they're glad they moved and feel they lead a rich, productive life with new friends. Why all the way to Bisbe? Because there was no waiting list.

Financial aid to house the elderly can be in the form of county, city or federal governmental assistance, grants and scholarships from philanthropic groups, or it's developed by non-profit sponsors —generally religious or civic organizations. Monetary aid from governmental agencies ranges from the 202 program of the Department of Housing and Urban Development, to high-rise apartment complexes dependent on a mixture of county, federal and corporate funds. The character of these multi-unit facilities varies widely— from well maintained, architecturally pleasing old mansions saved from the wrecking ball, to the dilapidated concrete tenements seen on the evening news.

To be eligible for 202 housing (also called Section 8 rental assistance, in which the rent is 30% of one's adjusted monthly income) a person must have income not higher than 50 per cent of

the median income for the locality. The local housing agency or HUD office can supply you with the appropriate income limits for your area because the figures vary from state to state. Facilities that accept low income Seniors may also take families and/or physically disabled, and in some developments, not all the units are subsidized, so you'll have people paying full market price alongside someone paying below market rate. Usually a percentage of the apartments or rooms are reserved for low income applicants. A current trend, borrowed from the Scandinavians, is housing multi-generational families together. When it works it's a beautiful sight—grandmothers playing with toddlers, and teenagers repairing walkers. Don't count on applying for an apartment one month and moving in the next, unless your best friend's the mayor or minister or both, as it can be a two or three year waiting list. Just as there's no typical Senior, there's no typical standard model of subsidized Senior housing. We've seen state-of-the-art facilities that are extremely well run with a caring devoted staff, and we've visited places where you'd be afraid to spend the night.

In some subsidized places meals are mandatory, recreational

activities and counseling are provided, as well as educational and wellness programs, and van transportation. In others, a shared room is about all you'll get, and dining comes from Meals on Wheels, a local food bank, or a can of Ensure and maybe a stale roll saved from a Senior Center lunch program. In rural areas, a civic group such as Rotary or a local church will "adopt" a facility, providing volunteers for transportation, outings, and enrichment programs. Depending on one's needs, you'll find subsidized housing offering Independent and Assisted Living. The units are often tiny and cramped, but with a housing shortage for the elderly, it's about all that's available.

The real challenge is unearthing what subsidies you or your parents might be eligible to receive. Statistics tell us there's a shortage of single-person units, while often a two-person apartment or room stays vacant because there are no eligible couples. If you're desperate to get a roof over your head, why not consider living with someone—you might get bumped up on the list like gangbusters, and make a new friend at the same time.

You're going to find governmental-assistance units through your HUD or Ombudsman office, but you should know that there is other subsidized housing available for Seniors. Your search can begin in the yellow pages, and then you have to be prepared to ask questions, bug people unmercifully, and be persistent. Don't overlook subsidized housing run by non-profit organizations and property management companies, and consider housing administered by "for profit" groups, which are subsidized by HUD funds and are often in better hands than the old bureaucratic, inefficient government. Check with your church, alumni group (some colleges, universities and professional schools offer stipends for healthy older alums in faculty housing), and spend some time inquiring about local do-gooder groups, called Benevolent Societies (i.e. Masonic Order, Odd Fellows). Kiwanis International, Little Sisters of The Poor, Jewish Federation and many others offer a helping hand to Seniors. Senior Centers and Senior Fairs are good resources for lists of retirement residences offering subsidies, as is the counsel offered by Geriatric case managers. Most housing in this category is short-staffed so a large percentage of residents have in-home care, often in the form of a caring family member.

A lot of profiteers have hopped on the Senior housing bandwagon by contracting with HUD to supply housing. They find old buildings, usually in run-down neighborhoods, and they are guaranteed a certain percentage of the monthly rent by the government. In turn, they are supposedly "helping the poor" Seniors. In reality, some of them are taking advantage of them. Scrutinize the places carefully and consider if *you'd* want to live there. Notice the condition of the buildings and the maintenance, and the quality of the food if it's offered. Ask to see a copy of the last HUD inspection— you might be surprised.

Here are some helpful questions to ask of the resident manager:

■ Is there a waiting list? How long? Must I make a deposit to get on the list? Is it all, or a portion? Is it refundable?

∎ Does the entry fee include ownership of the unit?

∎ Is there an initial amount owed prior to moving in? How much?

∎ What is the monthly rate? What does it include? Are there any extra charges?

∎ What happens if my income goes down? Or up?

∎ How many people does the monthly rate include? How many meals are included? Must residents pay for missed meals? Is there a charge for tray service if the resident is unable to go to dining room?

∎ Are guests permitted for meals? What is the charge?

∎ Are wheelchairs permitted in the dining room? Is there a separate dining room for Assisted Living?

∎ What's the alcohol/smoking policy?

∎ Do units with kitchens have ovens? Microwaves?

∎ Is there a cable hookup? How about pets?

∎ Can we bring our own furnishings?

∎ Are facilities available for overnight guests?

∎ What activities are offered? Classes? Outside entertainment?

▪ How close is public transportation? Shopping? Social, educational and religious activities?

▪ Is transportation provided by the residence?

▪ Is there an emergency call system in the units?

▪ Is physical therapy and/or occupational therapy available?

▪ Is health care available? Are you licensed to dispense medication? Is there a physician/nurse on call?

▪ If I need more care in the future do I have to move to a new unit? How much is that?

▪ Is there a trial period so I can try it for a week or weekend?

16.
Small Board and Cares

F inding out about board and care homes for the elderly in this country is not unlike deciphering hieroglyphics. The concept is clear—residential custodial care to the aged and disabled in a home that provides room, meals and some type of protective oversight supervision or personal care to residents. Yet, there's no such creature as a typical board and care home. These homes include places in which three residents share a home with Mrs. Jones, the operator, to a 1,400 bed facility. They range from bungalows in blue-collar neighborhoods that make it on the residents $592 SSI checks to Mediterranean-styled homes in affluent parts of town where four clients each pay $3,500 a month. These homes can also vary from those that have no staff with health care training, to facilities that provide daily nursing care with a licensed staff; and they include dreary old houses warehousing the elderly and frail in miserable conditions to attractive, innovative residential settings offering a high quality of long term care. Everyone agrees, it's a segment of Senior housing with little consistency.

And what a mixed bag of people small board and cares serve. They're differentiated by a variety of characteristics, including socioeconomic background and income level, age, overall health, physical limitations and mental condition. Many times, residents are mixed—a frail but sharp eighty-year old might be in a room with a 56 year-old Alzheimer's patient.

From a study of the Board and Care industry commissioned by AARP we found that states license board and care homes for ten people and fewer under more than 25 different names. A glimpse reveals:

> Domiciliary Care Facilities (Alabama)
> Adult Residential Care Facilities (Alaska)
> Rest Homes, Family Care Homes, Residential Homes
>   (Delaware)
> Shelter Care Facilities (Illinois)
> Family Care Homes (Kentucky)
> Boarding Care Homes (Kansas)
> Personal Care Homes (Pennsylvania)
> Basic Care Facilities (North Dakota)

In many states, such as North Carolina, they're called Homes for The Aged when licensed for more than six residents. Not only is there no common nomenclature, here's more to drive you nuts:

▌ Discrepancies in staffing level requirements, which affect daily operations in a care facility, are rampant. Bedridden or chairfast residents can get lost in the shuffle. About half of the states have minimum staffing requirements for board and care homes, but these minimums aren't related to the needs of the residents in a particular facility. Poor Aunt Ida, incontinent, blind, but able to recite Walt Whitman, could be unattended for hours if everyone was busy. In some places staffing levels are so low, in addition to having no guidelines for assessing residents' needs, that the elderly are neglected. Some states permit bedfast residents, although six impose conditions, while many states will let you stay if you're chairfast.

▌ Most state licensing agencies inspect the premises at least once a year, using nurses or social workers, but again, each state does it differently.

▌ And finding out who issues the licenses is a wild goose chase. Some states classify it under Department of Health and Social Services, and in Nebraska it's under the Bureau of Health Facility Standards in the Department of Health. In Oregon, where they're innovative and staffing levels are mandated for all board and cares, two of the three types of RCFs require residents to be ambulatory, and there are three separate funding sources available to residents. Everyone wants to hit the trail for Oregon. You get the picture — licensing is a bureaucratic red-tape nightmare and states have no conformity. Call the Ombudsman or Area Office of Aging to find out what's going on where you live.

▌ Many states do very little to identify unlicensed homes and/ or to require unlicensed homes to become licensed. AARP found agencies reported only 25 cases of taking court action against unlicensed homes in the year preceding the survey.

▌ Costs of board and care vary widely. About half of the elderly residents pay for their care solely with private resources. The monthly tally to residents spans a wide range, depending on location, services and amenities, and, also, what the traffic will bear. Mom'll be paying a lot more in San Francisco or Chicago at The Plastic Rose where she has a swell view than if she's living at Della's Crocheted Doilie in Schuyler, Kentucky. And there are subsidies available, too, but you have to unearth them. Oregon is praised for it's successful program whereby the state picks up the bill. Forty states and the District of Columbia offer State Supplemental Payments to SSI recipients, and personal needs allowances.

▌ While most states have laws prohibiting admission of a bedfast resident, little is known about how effective the physician review certification is. California is considering a ban on bedfast residents, while in Florida they're thinking about abandoning the prohibition. This brings up how residents could exit the building in emergency, and isn't it a risk for social isolation? Where states have different staffing requirements, they're focused on the size of the home rather than on the care needs of the resident. Many states stipulate that homes have "sufficient staffs to meet the needs of the residents," which is wide open for interpretation.

▌ Amenities in board and care homes is as varied as the homes themselves. Some "homes away from home" have a beautician on site, offer transportation to church and doctor appointments, and the residents appear coherent and self-sufficient as they intermingle, enjoy recreational activities and dine together in attractive surroundings. In others, the heat's cranked up to 85, everybody's snoozing, unaware of *I Love Lucy* blaring away on the tube, the plastic slipcovers have outlived their usefulness and the place reeks of stale urine.

▌ As the definition of board and care in most states refers to nonmedical community-based living arrangements that provide room and board and 24 hour supervision or personal care to residents, let's look at what this care actually is. People who need assistance with the activities of daily living will have someone to help with dressing, grooming, bathing, and eating, as well as those little things that the elderly find difficult, such as inserting a cassette, coping with a push-button phone, or opening the cat food can. Residents usually aren't allowed to cook in the kitchens, but often they're encouraged to participate by clearing dishes or performing small helpful chores if their health permits. Monthly rates generally include housekeeping, laundry, snacks and transportation. A random sampling of 50 facilities showed that they included restaurant and movie outings, excursions, an in-house beautician, game room, church outings, arts and crafts, and a shuttle to a nearby Senior Center.

When considering a small board and care, see if you can meet the owner or owners. This will tell you a lot. How involved in the daily operations are they? What's the staff turnover? Notice the overall condition of the residents—are they alert or are you in Zombie-land? Some of the best-run homes are owned and operated by Filipinos, and because of their natural caring, nurturing attitudes towards their elders, they often provide a warm loving home when it's needed most. Ralph was devastated when his high school sweet-heart Ruthie died after 61 years together. Never self- sufficient, he was unable to care for himself, but adamant in resisting the old folks home. When Doctor Bob noticed his skeletal appearance, he called Angelina's Haven, a cozy board and care he had recommended to another couple, and said he was bringing a friend over that afternoon. Ralph moved in pronto and has blossomed. And his nightly rendition of "Beer Barrel Polka" on the organ is more than what any doctor would order for the little old ladies.

Small board and care homes fill a definite need—they can help alleviate feelings of loneliness, the interaction can foster friendships, residents can frequently have their own furniture, and many have a home-like ambiance not found in nursing facilities. They're usually one-level dwellings with separate quarters for one or two live-in staff. And often it's less costly than a nursing home. But they have their drawbacks. You usually can't have guests for meals or to spend the night, in a lot of homes the clients are over- medicated and they sit around zonked out, and some of them are poorly run. Roberta was a wanderer, but her daughter was so anxious to have her "parked" somewhere so her life could get back to normal, that she neglected to see what security measures were in effect at the board and care. Imagine Roberta's panic when she received the dreaded call that Mom had gone for a stroll and was missing for two days before school kids found her asleep at the bus station. Be sure to ask tons of questions, such as, "How do you handle emergencies?" and keep your eyes and nose working when you visit. Is there somewhere to sit outside if Dad enjoys being outdoors? Can he still have a cigar somewhere? Sample a meal, see who's running the show, and check out the bathrooms.

17.
Sidestepping the Pitfalls of Moving

I f you have ever moved, you know it's high on the list of emotional experiences. The very perception of a move as an over-whelming ordeal is often critical in the decision to move. Older people get paralyzed with the thought, so they stay put and we kids don't push it because we don't want to clean out the attic and basement. In the confusion of a major move, the big picture is often too emotional and difficult for some Seniors to grasp. Older adults are likely to fixate on the trivia rather than deal with the emotions triggered by leaving a neighborhood and home of many years. Fretting over little things becomes a coping mechanism for many.

If your parents are alone and the move is beyond even you, you might try one of the following suggestions for help:

- retirement communities
- local churches
- real estate agencies
- service groups
- senior centers
- friends
- moving professionals
- Senior organizations, ombudsman
- professional organizers

If you follow a few simple guidelines, you can reduce the worry and stress, and remember, these suggestions apply to the Senior who is moving, as well as to their children who may be organizing the move. For those who are moving out of necessity, there could be added stress: loss of a spouse, failing health, financial difficulty, or the horrors of a natural disaster. We have found, in moving hundreds of Seniors, that it isn't the actual move that produces the stress as much as peoples' reaction to the move. Older adults have often lived in their homes for over thirty years, collecting tremendous amounts of stuff, and the very thought of weeding out and making decisions is mind-boggling. And, of course, it's difficult to decide what to take as you're undoubtedly moving to a smaller space, not to mention the emotional roller coaster you find yourself on. Statistics tell us that most people must dispose of more than 75% of their belongings before moving from the family home to a retirement community. Here is some food for thought to ensure a smoother move:

Planning ahead is important.

It's vital to plan ahead, so don't wait until the last minute. We can't stress this enough. You need time to make a concise list of what's being moved, stored, given away, thrown away, or sold. One way to ensure consistent bids from movers is to have a list of all the articles being moved. Give one to each of the moving companies so that the bids will be uniform. One of our clients decided at the last minute to take his grand piano, forgetting that the first two bids did not include it, so when the mover came to start the move and was told the piano was going, he had to raise his bid and to come back the next day because he needed more men and different equipment. Needless to say Mr. Travis was furious, but it was his fault because he had not told these particular movers about the piano. Most important in this process, give yourself ample time to go through your things, as parting with letters and treasures can be very difficult and time consuming.

Find a reliable mover.

Word of mouth brings best results, or ask the retirement community, if that is where you are headed. Ask a lot of questions of neighbors, friends, or family who may have recently moved. If you resort to the yellow pages, it's wise to call your local Better Business Bureau, and while they won't recommend a specific moving company, they will tell you if "Movers and Shakers" has had any complaints filed against them. If a moving company isn't affiliated with a larger one, it's wise to check them out thoroughly. Beware of moving trucks with no names, as some may not be licensed. A friend of ours, Mrs. Raskin, hired a moving company because they were the cheapest, and she didn't check them out. The day of the move the neighbors called the police because they saw an unmarked moving van, and men taking furniture out of the house. The police came, found out the movers were operating without a license and stopped the move. Our friend was left with some of her belongings on the lawn, and her house a mess.

Movers may charge whatever they want for a move. If a mover quotes a low rate and it takes him much longer than he had anticipated, unless you had additional boxes to pack or move, he must

stick with his price. Don't ever pay more than the contract if you were not responsible for the delay. The movers must eat it! Many older adults are not sure what their rights are. If you are charged more, tell them you will pay them what the contract stated and that you will check out the problem with your lawyer (even if you don't have one) and get back to them. That might just solve the problem. The Interstate Commerce Commission regulates moves across state lines, and if you want information about a long distance move, you can telephone them. A local move is 50 miles or less and is generally calculated by the hour. Long distance moves are over 50 miles and the price is determined by weight and mileage.

Discounts for Seniors.

Some moving companies offer free or discounted wrapping paper, tape, and boxes, and sometimes will deduct an hour off the bill. Make sure you ask because this information is not always volunteered.

Written estimates.

Get at least two . . . in writing! Be sure the estimate includes these important words: NOT TO EXCEED$$$. We've seen bids differ by thousands of dollars for the same move. Some movers will come in with a low bid to get the job and try to intimidate the Senior at the end of the move by asking for more. Sometimes movers take longer than they had estimated, so it might be important to check with the Public Utilities Commission in your area to find out just how much over the original estimate they can charge. They should not charge anything over the estimate, unless you have added additional items to be moved or packed. Familiarize yourself with the company's terminology. You might have to sign a change order, but never sign a blank one. If you do sign one, be sure it's prior to the move.

Paying for the move.

Discuss the method of payment in advance. Most companies prefer cash or a cashiers' check. Some will take a personal check or a credit card. And speaking of money, please remember to tip the movers if you think they did a good job.

Movers need to know the layout of the new home.
Coordinate the move with the people at the other end.

Have a floor plan of the new residence for the movers. The physical layout of the new home is extremely important in determining the cost of the move. How many steps are there? Is there a freight elevator, or even an elevator at all? If there is only one elevator, can the movers block off time to use it or do they have to share it with the building? What is the street size and access to the building or home? How far away from the entrance does the truck have to park? Are the movers required to lay down masonite to protect the carpets and floors? If you are moving to a retirement community, inquire about reserving the elevator on moving day well in advance. Usually new residents can move in only during the hours between 8:30 and 5:00, however some communities hours are 8:30–11:30 and 1:30–4:30. You don't want to ask the movers to wait another day to unload because you neglected to inquire about the move-in policies. Many retirement communities will coordinate the move for you, but be sure you give them adequate notice.

Guaranteeing space on the street for the van to park.

Know what to expect once the van arrives. If it must park on the street, you might be required to get a parking permit, or to obtain "No Parking" signs. If a permit is not required, you will still need to arrange to block off part of the street for the van to park. The closer the better as it saves time and money. Park some cars in the street the night before or put saw horses in the street. If you're lucky, no one will move them, but don't count on it!

Different types of moving insurance.

You should understand the differences in types of insurance your parents will need. Included in the contract is protection up to 60 cents per pound. To be eligible for this coverage, you must write

60 cents per pound per article on the contract in your own hand-writing and sign it. This is the minimum insurance available.

The second type of coverage is declaring the actual cash value of your goods. There is no minimum charge for this protection, but maximum is $6.70 per thousand dollars. The third type is full value protection, and there is no deduction for the condition or age of the object. There is a charge of $10.10 for each thousand dollars in this type of coverage. These intricacies of the insurance clause coverage are complex and wordy, and we advise you to get a thorough explanation and fully understand the implications before you make a decision. This is especially important in a long distance move. If deductibles are factored in, these rates would be lower.

General moving tips.

Be sure everything is labeled clearly—what stays if anything, what goes. Movers are not mind readers, and they're not there to decide what you should or should not take. If it takes longer because you are disorganized, it will cost you more. Furthermore, be sure all of the furniture you want to take will fit into your new home. You should measure both the space and the furniture before the move. Mrs. Bruce had a spinet piano which was almost 200 years old. She measured the space for it in her new home but didn't notice the heat vent on the wall. When the movers put it in it's allotted space, she became upset because she realized it couldn't stay there. There was no other place for it that was big enough, and if the movers left she would have no way of moving it herself. She eventually had the movers turn off the heater and had to have it relocated. This need not have happened.

Don't assume the movers will unpack or put furniture together. Some companies will give you free boxes, and many companies have used boxes which they sell for much less than the new ones, but you will need to inquire about them. If you pack boxes yourself, use butcher paper rather than newspaper. You will have far less cleaning when you unpack, to say nothing of your newsprint-free hands.

Moving valuables.

Many people prefer to pack valuables and family treasures themselves, but there is a downside. If you pack the boxes yourself, be aware that the moving company won't insure the contents if the box is not damaged but the contents are broken. Never pack jewelry and small valuables; carry them with you on your person, or better yet, when you open a bank account near your new home, leave those valuables in a safety deposit box until you are all moved in.

You won't have to give it a second thought during the confusion of the move.

Keeping track of what's in the boxes.

If they pack themselves, make an itemized list of the boxes' contents, and then number the boxes to correspond with the list. This way you avoid writing everything on the outside of the boxes (usually unreadable anyway), and they are ready for the person who will be unpacking. If movers pack your belongings, be sure they write on the box specifically what room it came from, and a clue as to what's inside. Example: Dining Room dishes. Don't hold your breath waiting for the movers to do this. They are notoriously bad about it. So make sure you ask them to write the room and, hopefully, some of the contents on the boxes.

Photographing my parents' prized possessions.

If you have antiques and valuable pieces, it will be worth your while to either photograph or videotape them prior to the move.

This way you have documented the condition of your possessions before they leave your home. You can even photograph the boxes with their numbers clearly visible, so you will have proof that there were actually that many boxes.

Deciding what to take.

First, you must decide what you can't part with emotionally. Then decide what you actually need and can use. From there determine how it's all going to fit. As you face downsizing, this is a good time to communicate openly with your children and relatives about letting them have the things that you can't take. What a wonderful feeling to know that your large table which belonged to your grandmother will be used by another generation.

However, some people get carried away with the thought of lightening their load, and give away too much before they move. We know many Seniors who offered their possessions to others, thinking they wouldn't use them in their new home, but upon moving, realized that they in fact wanted them. It's better to take more than you need, because trying to replace items you gave away can be costly and time consuming. Sometimes older adults will give things away and then discover they were worth more than they thought, so we suggest you consider having an appraiser come in and appraise your prized possessions. Consider Rose, who gave away her husbands' mining tools, only to discover later that they were one-of-a-kind antiques and worth thousands of dollars. The lucky new owner refused to give them back.

Disposing of my parents' unwanted belongings.

A few suggestions: children, relatives, and friends, garage or estate sales, auctions, newspaper ads, donations to charity, hauling in payment for work, and there are businesses that will come into your home and buy everything outright. But beware of these outfits, as some are not very reputable. Sometimes it's easier for an outsider to sift through your personal belongings, rather than children, as it's often traumatic and sad for offspring to face, and frequently the process creates family friction.

Allaying my parents' fears of the moving day.

Many people prefer to do the organizing up to a certain point and then hire someone to orchestrate the final part. This is fine if you've given yourself adequate time, and have someone capable and qualified in charge the day of the move. It's very important to have someone at the house to answer questions, and be there when the movers are packing and moving. That person, whoever it is, can do a final walk-through after the van has left to be sure everything has been moved, all the lights are turned off, and the house is locked. Have someone at the other end to show the movers where to unload and place furniture. Don't forget to empty the refrigerator and freezer. Movers won't disconnect gas dryers nor will they hook up washers, dryers, or ice makers. The good news is that you don't have to empty dressers or cabinets that contain non-breakables.

If Dad insists on doing his own packing it could be a disaster.

If possible, try and persuade Dad to let the movers pack most or all of his belongings. It doesn't cost that much more and it certainly alleviates worry and anxiety. If, however, your father insists he wants to pack, then that's just what he must do. We can't tell you how many times we've arrived at a clients' house the day of the move and found them walking in circles with their unpacked earthly possessions strewn about, pulling their hair out with the movers due to arrive any minute. It's not worth it. And we'll tell you the movers aren't crazy about it either. When the movers arrive and find Dad hasn't packed, the estimate will not be valid as they will need to charge for additional time and materials, if they even had them on the truck, and don't forget the move will take longer than quoted. A tip for making Dad feel involved. Each day give him some homework such as cleaning out one desk drawer. This has a tendency to get his mind off the big picture, which can be too much to think about, and gives him a sense of accomplishment.

BE SURE TO:

▌ Start getting your bids as far in advance as possible.

▌ Get more than one bid.

▌ Take care of yourself—don't lift heavy boxes. Isn't that what grandchildren are for?

▌ Get everything in writing. If you change something make sure it is changed on the contract.

▌ Be sure the phone is hooked up at the new home on the day of the move, and don't cancel the phone at the old house until after the move.

▌ It's better to take more of your favorite things than to take too little.

▌ Be sure you have an overnight bag packed with daily essentials like your Scotch and your toothbrush.

MOVING CHECKLIST

8 Weeks Before the Move (or Sooner)

▌ Select your moving day.

▌ Contact movers and get bids from at least two companies.

▌ Start using up frozen foods, canned foods, and cleaning supplies.

▌ If ordering new furniture, do it now and have it delivered to the new home.

6 Weeks Before the Move (or Sooner)

▌ Make sure the items you wish to take will fit into your new home.

▌ Make a list of everything you want to bring.

■ Make a list of those items you want to give to family and friends, sell, and give to charity.

■ Throw everything else away.

■ Before giving things away, if you have something you know is old and you aren't sure of it's value, have it appraised.

■ If some of your belongings are to be stored, make the necessary arrangements. Make a list of what each box contains instead of writing it on the box. Then number the boxes on all sides to correspond with your lists. When you need something, it will be easy to find the right box by the numbers. Include on your list the condition of the furnishings. Have the storage person look at the furniture, then sign your list. It is a good idea to take pictures of some of the better pieces.

■ If you live in an apartment building, inform the management of your move and reserve the elevator.

4 Weeks Before the Move

■ Send out rugs to be cleaned and furniture to be repaired.

■ Obtain a change of address kit form your local post office and start composing a list of address changes.

■ If needed, arrange for insurance coverage in your new home.

■ Contact utilities (water, garbage, telephone, cable, newspaper, utility company) and have them disconnect services at your old home the morning after your move and connect services (if needed) at your new residence the day of the move.

▌ If you are packing yourself, get boxes from the movers or elsewhere, start with items you won't be needing for a while.

▌ If you are renting, give your notice.

2 Weeks Before the Move

▌ Send change of address forms to the post office, magazines, financial institutions, doctors, lawyers, insurance companies, friends and family.

▌ Dispose of flammable liquids, paints, and poisons.

▌ Contact charities to set up a time for pick-up.

▌ Arrange for someone to clean your home after you have moved out.

One Week Before the Move

▌ Give away plants not to be moved.

▌ Pack items you wish to move yourself and label them.

▌ Have hauler come and take excess garbage and rubbish.

▌ If you are giving items to charity, have them pick up your items.

■ If relatives and friends are getting certain pieces, have them come to get them before the movers, if possible.

One Day Before the Move

■ Pack personal items you will need the night you move in.

■ Make sure everything is labeled and you are ready for the movers.

■ If living in a house, block off area of street in front of your house for the moving van.

■ Say good-bye to your neighbors. It can get very hectic for you and the movers if you wait until the moving day.

Moving Day

■ Prior to the arrival of the van, have cars out of the driveway and garage.

■ Have money or check ready for the movers.

■ Make sure someone is at the home to help direct the movers.

■ Remove jewelry and small valuable items from drawers and transport them with any important personal papers yourself.

■ Clean out refrigerator and freezer. Leave what you want the movers to pack.

- Have your personal items and bedding in your car, if possible, before the movers arrive.

- Have the plan for your furniture placement for your new home handy.

- If there are items left in your home you are not taking, have them labeled so the movers will not pack them.

- Do a complete house and yard check before the van leaves.

- Check all appliances to make sure they are off.

- Turn off heat and lights, and lock windows and doors.

- Leave keys inside for new owner or agent.

- Leave home only after van has left.

- Go out for lunch or dinner. This is where the kids, the community or a professional mover take over.

- Relax and rest.

- Have a cocktail and go to bed.

Address Change

- Drivers license
- Car registration
- Voter registration
- Magazines / Periodicals
- Credit cards
- Charge accounts
- Insurance
- Investments
- Finance companies
- Doctor, dentist
- Bank
- Accountant
- Catalogs
- Church or synagogue
- Cleaners
- Newspapers and periodicals
- Frequent flyer program
- Friends and relatives
- Utilities

18.

What To Know About Working With a Realtor or Contractor When Selling or Remodeling Your Parents' Home

W|e have orchestrated the moves of many Seniors, and it seems the same concerns are voiced almost every time. It's one thing to know about retirement communities and to have made a choice of where you may want to hang your hat, but actually saying good-bye to your home is quite another story. Most agents, brokers, and contractors are honest and reputable, but, as we all know, there are snakes in every profession. It's a great temptation for unscrupulous people to take advantage of Seniors, and in these two professions it seems to be an easy thing to do. The Seniors are often lonely, confused, and looking for that special friend to talk to and help them out. They're especially vulnerable if they run across someone who will listen, and many are intimidated because they don't know what questions to ask and don't understand the process of remodeling or selling a home. Many are women who've never had to deal with any sort of house problems and don't have a clue about where and how to start. The horror stories are endless. No one will ever know the extent to which this happens, as it is difficult to admit you or your parents were duped. Included in this chapter are some tips for selling your home. It's important to know how to find and work with a realtor, and how to work with a contractor to spruce up your home in order to maximize your profits, or if you decide to stay, to adapt your home to your physical needs.

Mrs. Kennely wanted to move. She had no relatives and not many friends to give her advice, so when she received a flyer in the mail from a real-estate agent she called him out of the blue. The agent, Mr. Barry, came over, looked at the house and told her on the spot what he thought it was worth. He never had any other agents come through for more input on price, and subtly began pressuring her into signing a contract three days later. After the house didn't sell, she found out the price had been so inflated in the beginning that even though they lowered it, her home still sat unsold for months. Before the contract expired she found a new agent. She had retained Mr. Barry solely on the basis of the price he had given her. Only one offer had come in during all this time, and she was being pressured again by Mr. Barry to pay for the termite work and all the inspections. Unbeknownst to Mrs. Kennely, he was also representing the buyer. He just wanted to make a quick sale and pocket all the commissions. Mrs. Kennely could have avoided months of aggravation had she started with a more reputable realtor.

The best way to find a realtor is through word of mouth. Talk to your friends and relatives, and interview at least two, preferably three, making sure you get solid references. Check out other houses in your neighborhood on the market and find out who is selling them. If you don't have anyone to give you a referral, then go to a large real estate company with a good reputation in your area. In most cases, Seniors get taken advantage of by a realtor working alone. If you decide to go that route, check him or her out carefully. In choosing an agent, you'll need to ask a few good questions. What are the addresses of the homes they have listed or sold in the last six months? What are the names and phone numbers of some of the recent sellers? What are the addresses of the homes they listed in the last six months that have not or did not sell? What price do they think you can sell your house for? Do they have a minimum listing time? How would they market your property if they got the listing? And, do they bring in other agents from their office to arrive at a realistic selling price? Find out if they have knowledge of your area, how long the average house they list is on the market, what the asking price was, and what the selling price was. This way you have a better chance to learn if the realtor prices the houses to sell. Also, does the realtor believe in open houses and if so, how many will they hold in a one month period?

We really don't advocate Seniors trying to sell their own homes or even listing them with so called cut-rate realty companies. The less responsibility you have, the less worry you have. Combined with the magnitude of the move, the added stress of coping with buyers yourself, and strangers tramping through your home without an agent to run interference, can be too much. A full service real estate company does absolutely everything if you choose one wisely. Some of the perks you get with going with a full service company are: broker's open houses, Sunday open houses, advertising in the newspaper, direct mail campaigns, brochures printed with the picture of the house, being on the Multiple Listing Service and, most important, a Comparative Market Analysis predicated on actual sales in your neighborhood in the last six months. Mrs. Kennely's story illustrated a potentially serious problem when selling a home, particularly when using an agent you don't know and one that's representing both the buyer and seller. It's possible for one person to represent both, but if you are the seller signing the contract then your agent has a fiduciary responsibility to you as the client. This means the relationship existing when good conscience requires one to act at all times for the sole benefit and interests of another, with loyalty to those interests. In other words, your agent should be going steady with you, not anyone else.

Determining a selling price can be one of the most difficult pieces of the puzzle when putting your home on the market. Mr. Smythe, after biting the bullet and deciding to move, wanted to know more about the process of selling his home before he contacted a realtor. He had lived in his house for 55 years and was totally unaware of what the procedures were once he signed on the dotted line. We suggested that he and his wife cruise the Sunday open houses in his area. He got the newspapers, circled the houses sounding comparable to his in size, and with his trusty map, set out. This way he could see what his competition was and get a little knowledge under his belt before meeting with his realtor for the first time. A note of caution: be sure you're comparing apples with apples. If a house similar in size to yours and in better shape with a fresh coat of paint is listed for $250,000, you may have to list yours for less if you've been putting off maintaining it for years because you wanted to play golf every Sunday.

Make sure you're not kidding yourself. Be realistic about the condition, and take off those rose colored glasses. A good agent will explain to you how they arrived at a certain price, and on what they based their decision. The most deceitful scam going is realtors working with Seniors who give them an inflated asking price just to get their business. Who would you pick, an agent who said your house was worth $250,000 or one that said $350,000? Remember, just because a man's house is his castle doesn't mean yours is one. Don't fall into the trap of becoming too emotionally involved with your house. It's only worth what someone will pay for it. This is called Fair Market Value, the highest price which the property would sell for in the open market. When you are given comps (prices for comparable homes in your area recently sold), check that the figures are for the selling price not the asking price, and that they are not older than six months. It can make a big difference how much you get for your house when it is listed. Prices fluctuate, so if you have a comp from a year ago, it may not hold water today. Remember, listing your house at the right time of year can directly affect the sale, so begin with a realistic asking price, understanding you might have to come down as much as 10% or more. If you get greedy and list too high, the house will sit, then become stale over time and you may have to lower the price even lower than what you could have sold it for had you been less hungry for the dollars. Remember, the seller sets the price after heeding the advice from his realtor. If you don't have any offers after one month, the price is probably too high. Listen to what he says. He is the expert. It all boils down to a good and trusting relationship between the seller and the agent. "If it's priced right, you can hope for multiple offers."

Depending on the time of year and market conditions in your area, it is advised to sign a contract for no longer than 90 days. The average time it takes to sell a house, depending on the area, is about three months and the normal (if there is any such thing) escrow is usually 45 days. Don't be pressured into signing for a longer period of time unless you are very confident in your agent. If an agent does pressure you, that's a warning signal, so pay attention! If you decide to break the contract before it expires, be sure there is no penalty clause stating that you can't put your house back on the market in the same time frame or with a different agent. The most common type of contract is the Exclusive Right to Sell listing, where the agent will get the commission no matter who brings in the buyer. A reserve clause is one which enables the seller to have a list of potential buyers who would be excluded from any contract with the agent. You must have these in writing so they are documented if one decides to buy the house. Forget trying to tell the realtor after the fact that this person was someone you knew.

Let's talk about the commission. In almost every circumstance, it's 6% of the selling price. This is, however, not written in stone. It can be negotiated. Make sure you have included everything you want your agent to do in the contract because memories can be short. If it's not in the contract, you may be disappointed. Mary Nell wanted her house open every Sunday, but neglected to state it in the contract. She just assumed that was the standard practice. After the contract had been signed she talked with her agent about when she would start the open houses. The agent told her she didn't believe in them. Oh well!

A good agent will explain how the offer will work. The buying agent will want to sit down with you to present the offer. Most agents will not do it on the phone. Once you have heard the offer and an hour long history of the buyer and his family, there are three ways to respond: accept it, refuse it, or make a counter offer. Be prepared to deal and try to keep emotions from getting in the way. Mr. Tuck told us he was insulted by the offer on his house. I told him he should realize that the buyer is going to try and get the house for as little as he can, so making a lower offer isn't out of line. It can be too low, and if that happens, your agent will tell you what to do. When it sells, make sure you get a big enough deposit at signing time. If the buyer backs out after all the contingencies are lifted, you are entitled to keep the deposit. This is especially important if you have already moved to a retirement community. If you have a mortgage on your house, you will be paying two monthly payments until the house sells again. Your agent should explain to you the 72 hour release clause, which states that if the seller receives another offer which is satisfactory, the buyer is given 72 hours to remove his contingencies, or he must withdraw his offer. The most common types of contingencies a prospective buyer will stipulate are loan approval, sale of buyer's house, structural inspection, termite inspection, roof and furnace, asbestos, and lately a property inspection, looking for that buried fuel tank.

You can sell your home "as is", but it certainly helps to jazz it up a bit. With Seniors, the years of collecting bottle tops, string, rubber bands, Life magazines, and every size box you can imagine can add up to a massive accumulation of junk. Throw it all out, put things away, tidy up the place, and take the knee-highs off the shower rod in the bathroom. When the house is being shown, keep

it neat and clean. Your agent will need to have a key, and will put a lock box on the front door so other agents can have access to the house. With an "as is" sale, you are still required to disclose all the problems you know about your house, and that means everything. One of our clients was sued and lost because she did not disclose dry rot she didn't even know about. If you are unsure of the answer when filling out the disclosure form, then put "unknown."

Another client decided to have her own structural inspection. When she received the report, she was stunned to learn she needed a new furnace, and to complicate matters there were major problems with her foundation. Because she ordered the report, she was required to disclose the whole thing to any potential buyer. Let the buyers pay for their own inspections. Usually the seller is responsible for the termite work, but again it's always negotiable. Remember, even though the buyer may have multiple inspections, the seller is not required to pay for any of the work. Now's the time to consider a home warranty, which would protect you in case something major is discovered which is a big surprise. You won't have to pay for the repairs.

Hurrah, you've sold your house and now it's time to close escrow. The escrow is done through a title company, usually of the buyer's choice. It is the time period between the lifting of all contingencies (getting a green light on the sale) and the actual money changing hands. Don't be surprised at the closing costs you, the seller, will incur. Many people are shocked by this, so again a good agent will let you know in advance what the approximate costs will be. Negotiating with title companies is also possible. A word of warning; title companies make mistakes too, so check your final escrow papers carefully before signing. Mr. Stover just signed his name where he was told after briefly looking at the document. He took the papers home and proudly showed them to his son. After reading them, his son discovered a $1,600 error in the pro-rating of the mortgage payment. The shorter the escrow time for most Seniors, the better they seem to operate. Basically it has to do with less time to worry. One last point: don't count your house sold just because you have a signed contract. It's not over until you have that big fat check in your hot little hand.

Getting your house ready to put on the market can be the biggest hassle of all, unless you've been a tidy paws and gotten an "A" in home maintenance. You'll just have to heave a lot of stuff you didn't think you could live without. Fixing your home up for sale can result in a much higher sale price but you'll need a little money and a lot of patience. If you're sick, don't have much available cash, can't stand the disruption, or have no one to help you, then don't bother. It's just not worth it. However, if the cash is the big problem, you can get a low interest home equity loan to foot the bills. If you think you can be on top of the situation, then you must be objective when looking at the condition of your home. Listen to advice from professionals about what you should do to the house. Hiring someone in the business can save you time and stress, and can even make you money in the long run.

Here are a few hints to help you make the most out of a tired house. Start with cleaning out all the unwanted belongings, unclutter the house, clean out the basement, garage and attic if you have one. Straighten out the closets. It always adds to the charm and curb appeal of the house to have some color around the front, so plant some inexpensive flowers in planters and in the yard. A fresh coat of paint never hurt, and at the same time hire someone to clean the windows. A more major expense would be to install a new carpet and draperies. And if you really get going, you can do a facelift on the kitchen and bathrooms, as these are two of the areas that can make a big difference in the sale. If you decide to remodel, do everything in neutral tones. Your own taste shouldn't be involved as much as making the house appeal to the most people. Don't try and make a personal statement. Also, if you are a smoker, take this habit outside for a few weeks. Consider that this stench affects many people in a negative way, as do animal odors.

Now you're ready to sell. If you decide to sell it yourself, even though we do not advise it, make sure you have all the papers you'll need, such as sales contracts and disclosure forms. Have an attorney look over any papers before you sign them, and know you will have to pay the buyer's agent around 3% of the sales price. Good luck, it's not bad if you're organized and have friends with lists of people to contact.

You will probably have to work with a contractor if you decide to remodel your home to fit your future needs, or if you decide to do a facelift on the old house before you sell. To avoid costly, nerve-wracking, and time- consuming mistakes, get three references when choosing your contractor. You will want to know what his last jobs were, and the addresses and phone numbers of those jobs. If he won't give you this information, don't hire him. Only people who have worked with a contractor know how that contractor works and the quality of that work. Call the references, identify yourself, and ask if you can see the work the contractor did. Ask if the work was completed on time, was within the budget, if they were satisfied with the work, and if the contractor did what he promised to do. Make sure they have insurance and worker's compensation. Mrs. Thomas' roof had leaked for years, but with a dying husband and her own frailty, the roof was put on the back burner. After her husband died she needed a project, so she decided to fix her roof and all the damage to her beautiful wallpaper and molded ceilings. The very next day she had someone knock on her door from Trustee Roofing, who said they were offering a deal in her neighborhood for two days, so if she wanted to have any work done she had to sign up now. She hired him on the spot. Before he left he had a signed contract of sorts in his pocket and one half the amount of the work in his hot little hand. The very next day he arrived with two men, spent about four hours on the roof, then asked for the final payment, even going so far as to give her an official looking warranty. Mrs. Thomas then painted and wallpapered the living and dining rooms and had the warped hardwood floor repaired. Can you guess what happened when the first rain came? The living room flooded, the wallpaper was ruined and Ralph the roofer was enjoying a beer on the beach in Acapulco, thanks to Mrs. Thomas. She later called a roofer that a friend recommended to her and found out, to no one's surprise, that nothing had been done to the roof to the tune of $5,000. Listen up! Seniors get ripped off more times than the general public.

When you start the process of getting your bids, be very sure that each bid is for the exact same work and materials to be used. A good way to guarantee this is to write everything down that you want done, being clear in specifying the brands to be used. Give each contractor a copy so there will be no misunderstanding. Be sure to keep one for yourself. If you do not know what brands you want, ask the contractors to show you pictures or tell you where to go to see the items on display. Be aware that there is a wide range in the prices of all materials, so be careful on this point. A good contractor will present you with a detailed contract, spelling out quality of materials, work to be completed, payment schedule, and length of time to complete the job. You can even add a clause to the contract stating that if the work is not completed in the allotted time, he must start paying you. This is a good incentive for the contractor to finish the job on time. Try not to pay more than 10% down to start the job and never agree to buy tools as part of the job unless you want them for yourself. Look at the situation carefully if a contractor wants more money before it's due. Always leave enough money unpaid until the job's finished so the contractor will not walk away, and don't pay off the contract if you are dissatisfied with the work. Make the contractor fix any problem before you pay, because if you don't, you may never see him again.

Permits can be tricky, depending on where you live. If a home-owner does not specify that he wants a permit, sometimes contractors will skirt the issue because the permit fee comes out of the contractor's pocket. There are financial consequences in not getting a permit, and can result in the city not letting you do the work. Most cities also charge a penalty fee on top of the permit fee if you

are caught. If it is major work to be done, you'll need the permit for resale anyway, so bite the bullet. Remember, only a contractor with a license or the owner-builder can get a permit, so if someone says you don't need a permit, ask to see his license if you haven't already. Be very careful of "time and materials" jobs. If you opt for this, ask for a "not to exceed" price. Sometimes it's hard for a contractor to give you a fixed price if he can't see the extent of the job, but if you can get a fixed price do it, especially if you haven't worked with the contractor before. One last thought: pay only the contractor, not the people who work for him. It's his responsibility, not yours. We had a case where an older gentleman was intimidated by the sub-contractor because he said it was Friday and he needed the money for his wife and kids for the weekend. The older man had already paid the contractor, but the contractor hadn't paid his subs. The old man fell for it. Don't, it's not your problem.

All this may sound overwhelming, the selling of the house and the remodeling, but it can go smoothly if you remember these few points: it's your house, your project, take control, do your homework, and remember these people all work for you and you're the boss of yourself!

19.
Help!
I Can Hardly Cope With My Own Life, And Now My Parents Are Falling Apart!

O
ne of the most difficult situations a person will face is the mental and/or physical deterioration of his parents. So many factors are involved—and most are totally foreign to children. Working offspring often experience more stress coping because of time constraints and demanding job responsibilities. Donna Wagner of the National Council on Aging warns, "You can be competent in every other part of your life and be blowing this one." According to Dr. Andrew Scharlach, Professor of Aging at the University of California, Berkeley, "The number of people 85 and older who rely on their children will nearly double by 2030, and will more than triple, says the census bureau, with families providing 80% of needed long term care." A recent survey by the Department of Health and Human Services found that half of all working Americans care for dependent relatives, and that nearly three quarters of these caregivers occasionally stay home from work to do so.

When the topic of our aging parents crops up, one senses the frustration and lack of control which can be devastating to families on many levels. Children ask, "How can I manage with the pressure of having to take time from work to deal with my parents? Is it possible to sell my parents' home, find them a place to live, decide what and what not to take, disperse their belongings, and move them all in a short time—with no help?" And who among us can comprehend the Medicare and supplemental insurance labyrinth? An overriding problem, which erodes the relationships between most children and their parents, is lack of communication. In most of the following situations, good communication could have eliminated many of the problems that confront families, the majority of which are uncomfortable to address. Also, the lack of centralized information easily available to the general public is a major stumbling block to children caring more effectively for their parents.

"Is there anything a family can do about siblings disagreeing on the care of their parents, and the fact that the burden of responsibility is not shared equally?"

Yes, there is. Meet the three Valentino children who lived in different cities across the country. When Mom had a stroke, the kids realized that a move to a retirement community was the best solution for both their parents. Convincing their father was the major hurdle, as he was healthy, and envisioned retirement communities as a "dead-end for Blue Hairs." The children said they would check out the available choices and present their findings to their parents. After much discussion, Mom and Dad decided to move to a Lifecare facility. Gina oversaw the remodeling of the apartment, while Bella sorted through 35 years of her parents belongings, interviewed and hired the movers, and helped her sister create a cozy new home for their parents. Dino, a financial wizard, did all the paperwork. The

children divided the responsibilities according to ability, desire and convenience, not forgetting what was best for Mom and Dad.

There always seems to be one child who bears most of the burden of care, and this child often harbors resentments at being "stuck." Where there's a geographic difference, two things have to happen. The siblings living nearest the parents must be able to ask for support, and those far away must be available. Support can be as simple as a phone call to your sister assuring her of your concern for Mom. Also, in our era of modems, faxes and expanded data bases, much of the legwork can be accomplished electronically. What's best for the parents should be the children's prevailing concern. Sometimes children have to make a decision on behalf of their parents which may not be ideal for all, but it's the only way to go. Siblings must adopt a give-and-take attitude and communicate honestly. Be prepared for personality clashes and outbursts of emotion that may have lain dormant. If you're feeling used, say it! If this doesn't work, find a good listener/ therapist such as a minister, social worker or best friend. This is a common problem, resulting in the emergence of support groups for family caregivers, and you can find them through Elder Care service groups.

Take the case of a sister and brother, Liz and Skip, who shared the responsibility of their elderly Aunt Arlene's welfare. As the aging

Aunt became more forgetful and confused, Liz kept a constant supply of companions on the scene to help with daily routines. Liz paid these companions, and tipped them generously. After all, her Aunt had begged to stay in her own home. When Skip found out that his sister was using their aunt's funds (eventually to be his), he fired off nasty letters to Liz chastising her for squandering their Aunt's money. Too bad they all hadn't talked it over before Arlene began to slip—they could have devised a workable plan, remained friends and supported each other emotionally.

According to Senate hearings, the majority of "unpaid caregivers are women, usually widows, daughters, or daughters-in-law. Caring for a frail friend or family member places severe emotional and physical strain—and to a lesser degree a financial strain on the caregiver."

"My parents need to make some decisions about their lives but are unwilling to face the problems. They are in denial about their aging–can we children take the decisions out of their hands, and if so, when is the appropriate time?"

Good question, and the answer is a resounding "yes." Sometimes it's not only advisable but necessary for everybody's well-being to assume the responsibility for parents' decisions.

Meet Pete and his mother Mary, a classic case of the all-American son who just couldn't face the fact that dear old Mom was losing it, and that he needed to step in and make some decisions.

When he finally took a good look at his mother's affairs, he was shocked to discover she hadn't paid household bills, her driver's license had been suspended, and she hadn't filed any IRS returns in three years. She pleaded with her son to let her remain in charge, and he acquiesced. After all, he rationalized, how can you buck your own mother? The situation went from bad to worse; neighbors noticed uncollected garbage, Mom's physician called to report that she was malnourished, and the final straw was when the cop stopped at his house to see why Mom was wandering around Walmart confused at 11:30 at night. Had he heeded the warning signals earlier, he might have avoided the $3,000 a month he's now coughing up for Mom to be in an Alzheimer's unit. If Prudent Pete had purchased a long term care insurance policy when Mom was in better health, she would have had coverage for a caregiver at home. The family lawyer had suggested it, but Mom was of the "it'll never happen to me" school. Don't tell Pete Mother knows best.

Pride, ego and trust are major players here because the issues are losing control, and giving in—part of the old parent/child conflict. Parents have to think they are part of the process, but at the same time they need to trust their child's instincts. "Seniors who made the decisions themselves were much more successful in their new living arrangements than those who did not. They were happier and the transition was smoother," according to a leading Elder attorney, William Kapp. There are several red flags generally accepted in the legal world to determine the ability of your parents to make life decisions.

■ Can the person make and express any choices concerning his/her life?

▌ Are the outcomes of these choices "reasonable"?

▌ Are these choices based on "rational" reasons?

▌ Is the person able to understand the personal implications of the choices that are made?

▌ Does the person actually understand the implications of those choices?

These questions may be broken down into two elements. First, does the individual have the capacity to assimilate the relevant facts, and second, can the parent appreciate or rationally understand his or her own situation as it relates to the medical facts?

"How can I become prepared for the emotional, physical and financial burden of caring for my parents? I feel so lost."

You might not be able to be prepared for the emotional impact of physical and mental deterioration. However, the financial and physical burden can be eased if you've planned carefully. Take action, try talking with them about their situation, so when the time comes you'll have a plan to implement. Start by educating yourself about the aging process—certain changes are normal and others are warning signs, and you need to know the difference to be able to make sound decisions. Review your parents' health status; have a heart-to-heart with their doctors and ask specific questions, such as, "What's the prognosis for my Dad's macular degeneration?" Older people are often unaware of newer medical diagnostic tests and home procedures. They don't want to inquire, fearing the worst, or they don't want to bother anyone. Acquaint yourself with the laws in their state that would apply to them, such as what is required to obtain a durable power of attorney, permitting you to make all their financial decisions should they become incapacitated. Don't be shy about asking your parents if they'd like your help with financial matters, and even if they're unwilling to share their information, it can pay off to investigate on your own. Unpaid bills, sloppy checking account records, old dividend checks and disregarded notices are signs they're not taking care of things, all slip-ups that could result in disaster such as insurance cancellation. Ada told us, "It's too confusing with these changed tax laws, new names on old banks, and fancy computers that write me letters—I just don't open my mail any more."

Be sure to take care of yourself—be organized and accept the fact that your needs are important. Look into using volunteers, nursing organizations, religious groups, service clubs, and cities and counties with outreach programs for families with elderly relatives. Know what's available in your parents' community before you need it.

"What changes might I see in my parents as they age?"

For many there are noticeable changes in their mental and

physical capabilities. Some become emotional—angry, hostile, afraid, depressed and despairing. We've seen many Seniors blossom and turn into real characters. There are no predictors in the aging process, but there are patterns. Often there is mental deterioration, and you should be prepared for this. For the lucky families, parents slip into their later years with ease, a good attitude, a sense of humor, and acceptance of the aging process. Often, as a person slows down physically and mentally, he or she is angry at the loss of control over their faculties. Most people over 65 experience some loss of hearing, sight, and memory, and gerontologists say it's quite common to hear complaints of chronic fatigue, insomnia, heart and blood pressure problems, and incontinence. Once older people accept the inevitable decline, frustrations subside, and a new peaceful attitude prevails. Rhoda fought her kids' advice and lashed out at family members because she detested losing her independence. Actually, she was afraid, because she was aware of her increasing dementia and knew that soon she'd be incapable of making her own decisions. When she finally was moved to an Assisted Living community, and had absolutely no memory, she began to relax. Here comes Rhoda six months later, she's in good humor and has formed the "Out To Lunch Bunch," and doesn't have the foggiest notion who's in charge.

Some men and women become overly emotional, hostile, afraid, dependent, reclusive, and revert to child-like ways. A physician reports that many older patients display symptoms of depression, others give up, and are riddled with despair.

"Sometimes I feel so scared when I think about my aging parents, that I wonder if this is normal? "

Yes, it is. You should bear in mind that children often haven't confronted the following:

- Fear of parents living versus dying.
- Fear of major illness.
- Anger at past events.
- Frustration at inability to tell parents what to do.
- Role reversal.
- Fear of losing a parent.
- Fear of losing the security of a family situation.
- Fear of being the older generation.
- Resentment at being trapped in the sandwich generation.
- Sadness at what is happening to parents' lives and yours.
- Making promises you know you can't keep.
- Too much responsibility.
- Fear of your own mortality.
- Inevitability of aging.
- Guilt for having the above feelings.

"What are some concerns my parents may be feeling as they age?"

These are very real to your parents, and you should consider that they might be experiencing:

- Fear of being a burden.
- Fear of death.
- Fear of not being able to care for themselves.
- Fear of being alone.
- Fear of living too long.
- Fear of outliving their money.
- Fear of being unable to enjoy the quality of life they always had.
- Fear of being a vegetable and lingering.
- Fear of losing a spouse.
- Fear of outliving friends.
- Fear of losing their minds.
- Fear of losing control of their lives.

One way children can bring up uncomfortable topics is to encourage parents to talk about their feelings when they lose their friends, neighbors or colleagues. We had a client who told his father, "I heard Fred died. You must be feeling very sad. He was such a great guy. I see the memorial service is next Wednesday, and I'd like to take you." Don't act as if these strokes, illnesses and deterioration are nothing. They are terrifying reminders that it happens every day, and by children acknowledging fear, shared sadness, and even relief that a person has died, channels of communication can be opened.

"Is it appropriate to discuss my parents' wishes for their burials?"

Yes, if it feels right—it depends on the situation. We've known many who sat down and planned their own burial, then sent the plan to their children. What a wonderful gift to be given as a child—you know you'll be doing for your parents exactly what they wanted, and it relieves you of the burden and emotional repercussions that are inevitable following the death of a parent, as well as the details of their demise. When parents indicate that they don't want to discuss the issue, it can lead to in-family fighting at a time when people should be coming together.

The Strongs weren't a close family and had never shared much of anything with each other, so when Earl Strong died unexpectedly, the family fell apart. The only son was paralyzed with guilt at not having made peace with his father. Mother, clinging to an era when women let men take care of everything, didn't even know how to write a check, let alone plan a funeral. Enter the son's girlfriend who sized up the situation and took control. She tackled the mountains of insurance paperwork, chose the casket, organized the service, and planned the party. When it was over, Mother remarked to girlfriend Jean, "It wasn't what Earl would have wanted, and he never liked deviled eggs anyway." Had they planned ahead, Earl's favorite artichoke canapes might have been relished by all.

Planning in advance has many advantages—the major one being that you are better prepared for a sudden death. Often, under emotional stress when one isn't thinking clearly, confusion reigns and it's easy to be taken advantage of. There's little time to compare prices, no time to consider the wishes of the deceased, and tension and family disagreements are heightened. Children often feel guilty when parents die, and they're likely to spend three times as much on burial arrangements because they're worrying about doing the best possible thing. At your parents' ages, the deaths of friends and colleagues are a common occurrence, and while they may not bring it up, you can look for an opportunity to discuss their situation at an appropriate time. Nearly every cemetery has a Family Service Counselor to help with pre-need arrangements, and you can encourage them to fill out the booklet, "What My Family Should Know" available through the American Cemetery Association. Some parents want no part of any discussion pertaining to death, and if that's the case, suggest they do it on their own and let someone know how it's being handled. We knew of a feisty octogenarian who refused to discuss anything about his finances with his family. His son, scanning the paper, casually announced, "Just listen to this—Herb Smileypuss down at the club didn't even have a will, they couldn't probate his estate, the paperwork took four years and now his heirs owe the IRS $36,000." The mere thought of the government getting more than its share prompted Grampa to ask his banker to recommend an estate planner.

"Where are some good sources to find out about Medicare, Medigap and Medicaid?"

We found it very difficult to get all the information in one place. Medicare payments are the same all over the country, the only difference is what the doctors charge for services, and whether or not they accept Medicare. Telephone any hospital, look in the phone book under United States Government, Health and Human Services Department, call AARP, or the National Association of Professional Geriatric Care Managers. Local Senior Centers usually can refer you to the appropriate offices if they don't know the answers. An invaluable source for easy-to-understand books on estate planning is Nolo Press in Berkeley, California. Their sixth edition of Social Security, Medicare and Pensions by Joseph L. Matthews, is clear, concise and probably can lower your frustration level considerably. Telephone them at 800-992-6656 to request a book, and also their catalogue.

"What documents and forms of my parents affairs are important?"

They should have several papers in place before they actually need them, so that another person can step in to make decisions should the need arise. Check out durable powers of attorney, durable powers of attorney for health care, durable powers of attorney for financial management, living wills, guardianships, conservatorships, a basic will, and living trusts, to mention a few. If your parents don't have any of these relatively simple arrangements in place and they become incompetent, you might have to go through a costly and emotional court process to be named their guardian. If you don't have an estate planner or attorney, call your local Bar Association for the referral of a lawyer who specializes in Elder Law, or the National Academy of Elder Law Attorneys. The Institute of Certified Financial Planners will give you a listing of three Certified Financial Planners in your area. Their toll-free number is 800-282-PLAN. You can also look for volunteer legal services to help you, or state agencies and consumer groups. We suggest writing to AARP, as they have many resources available. Most of these forms are not complicated, and many are available in a book entitled, *The Power of Attorney Book.* Also, many standard forms can be purchased in stationery and book stores. Here's the most ideal case:

A. Parents have joint savings and checking accounts with a child so that he has access to funds if necessary for an incapacitated parent.

B. Parents have shared their personal data with their children, updating financial records, health proxies, and wills regularly. When a parent dies, the child knows exactly what to do, and can expedite matters.

C. Parents have given copies of important documents to a lawyer or responsible person in addition to the child. If your papers are in a Safety Deposit Box at a bank, and your children aren't co-signers, there could be a problem after the parent's death. Usually the box is sealed and can't be opened unless the executor or administrator of the estate has been appointed, or in the presence of an Inheritance Tax Department representative.

"Is it OK to ask my parents the location of their valuables, safe deposit boxes, money, checking accounts and real property?"

Yes, it's not only appropriate, it's using good common sense. You might, however, not get the answer you hope for. The government has millions of unclaimed dollars because heirs didn't know they were left any money. If your parents are smart and want to make good long term plans, they will let you know what's available. Ask them to make a list that will include life, property, accident and health insurance policies, banking and investment information, credit card accounts, real estate records, and the whereabouts of valuable personal effects. Also, if one parent pre-deceases the other, you might have to help the survivor claim Social Security or other benefits, which aren't paid automatically. Mom may be too distraught to help you locate a copy of her marriage certificate, and she could conceivably go months unable to collect monies because no one can produce necessary documents. Start by getting all your ducks in a row, so you can help them make sound decisions concerning their future. If you're in the dark about their assets, how can you possibly help them if they need it? Some parents worry that if they share the information, the kids might take the Concorde to Paris for dinner and leave them at Denny's.

Pamela's father had a sizable estate, yet didn't really know what he had, as he was very disorganized. At one point he even sent a treasure map to Pamela, indicating how to find money he had buried under his house. She tried for months to get him to let her organize his papers, or help him find someone who could, but he wouldn't hear of it, thinking, "She just wants to get her hands on my hard-earned money." Only when he had a serious heart attack and didn't even know if he had insurance because he couldn't find the papers, did he let his daughter help. She hardly recognized poor old Dad confined to a bed in the public ward because no one had a clue who this man was and what coverage he had.

Ida, who hired us to help her move, told us her important papers and valuables were in her lawyer's hands. The day the auction people came to take some antiques, we asked if she had checked all the compartments for treasures. She replied "yes," but double-checking often produces something. Guess what was in the hidden drawer of one of the desks? A diamond and emerald ring valued at more than $100,000. Eventually we found other things concealed around the house, because she hadn't kept a record of where she'd stashed things and she simply forgot. This hide-and-seek game is popular with those of us who can't be bothered trekking to the safety deposit box, are suspicious of household help, or who don't trust their prized possessions to anyone.

"Can an outsider be more effective dealing with my parents?"

In many cases, someone who isn't close to the family has a much easier time coping with parents and can sometimes make more of an impact. A neutral person isn't emotionally involved, doesn't have a vested interest in the outcome, and without a personal history with the individual, can therefore usually be more objective. The outsider has more likely been involved in similar situations before, so he or she knows how to communicate with older adults effectively. Many times our parents respect a professional's advice and listen more attentively than if it were their own children. And often, parents and kids don't get along. If this is the case, it's doubly hard to work with the parents. Lastly, children sometimes resent their parents for consulting an outsider, as it implies that sons or daughters aren't as competent.

We were asked by a 55 year-old woman to clean out her mother's apartment because, "I just couldn't handle it emotionally." When we went to the apartment the first day, we were surprised to find it looking as though someone had just stepped out for milk. The mother was in a nursing home and wasn't expected to return home, and the daughter hadn't been to the apartment. We spent a week going through everything, and each night we called the daughter to report our progress. When we remarked to the daughter that it was too bad it was so painful for her to see her mother's place, to our surprise she retorted, "It's not painful at all. My mother and I don't see eye to eye, and I didn't want to have anything to do with her."

"Should I be considering long term care insurance for my parents as well as for myself?"

Having seen many Seniors dip into savings to pay for nursing homes, we think it's worth exploring. Studies tell us that 43% of all Americans who turn 65 this year will enter a nursing home sooner or later, and many more will require paid help to continue living at home. Consider that a year of care in a nursing home can average between $30,000 and $60,000 and you can see how easy it is to wipe out a lifetime dream. A large number of retirees have saved enough to provide a moderate retirement income, but as costs rise, many middle income Americans are shocked to find their parents' savings depleted. Long term care insurance is a specific insurance to help cover the costs of care for a chronic illness, such as Parkinson's disease, arthritis, Alzheimer's disease, or an injury that doesn't necessarily require continuous hospitalization. Often, it's defined as nursing home care, but it's important to realize that long term care is also provided in the home, and the services can include household chores or personal care services not provided by a health care professional. A good rule of thumb: if you have assets (not counting your car and house in excess of $50,000), and your income exceeds $25,000 annually, consider consulting a trusted estate planner to inquire about long term care insurance planning. The younger you are when you buy it, the cheaper it will be.

"Should we as children be discussing the distribution of our parents' possessions while they're still alive?"

Yes, if the parents aren't threatened by it. It certainly saves much agony and hurt among the children, and can help bypass many family squabbles. There are several things you as children can do. Ask your parents if they have any particular person they'd like to inherit specific items, and if the answer is "yes," suggest that it be put in writing and kept for safekeeping. Some parents resent their children meddling, but more often the kids want to know where they stand. Most parents appreciate it when younger relatives express an interest in family treasures, and they're eager to recount the histories of their prized possessions. Isabel had three children and she had them come to her house one day together. The eldest got to pick first, and he labeled his item with his name on a piece of tape on the underside. An impartial person recorded who got what, and after each child finished choosing, they signed the list, had copies made, and Isabel gave a copy to her lawyer.

"How can I hide my parents' assets before they are forced to spend down?"

Many of the Medicare and Medicaid rules are subject to state implementation and can differ substantially around the country, so it's best to check with a lawyer or an estate planner in your state, but here are a few basic guidelines. In determining resources available for Medicaid assistance, the following are not counted:

■ Your home, regardless of value.

■ Household belongings, furnishings, personal effects, and jewelry (some states limit the value of these items).

■ Burial plots for the individual or members of the family.

■ A burial account of up to $1,500 in most states.

■ Cash value of life insurance policies, provided the face value doesn't exceed $1,500 and term policies.

■ One automobile of any value in most states for use by the individual and his family.

■ Inaccessible assets of any value (meaning irrevocable trusts).

■ IRA, Keogh and pension funds.

■ Some states allow a person to retain certain income-producing property that is "essential to their self-support."

All other assets of the individual or couple are non-exempt assets. Since 1989, a couple's assets are combined for eligibility purposes and the non-applicant is allowed to keep between $12,000 and $60,000, depending on state law, subject to inflation. For the hospitalized spouse, his or her share of nonexempt assets have to be reduced to no more than $2,000. Transfers of assets and gifting to non-spouses has to begin 30 months prior to hospitalization for Medicaid to kick in, and in some states, if your parents are receiving Medicaid, a lien might be put on their residence when they die to help reimburse the state's expense. The government is starting to crack down on people who give away their or their parents' assets to heirs so they can qualify for Medicaid Coverage. A new law makes it a federal crime with a fine up to $10,000 and one year imprison-

ment for disposing of assets in hopes of getting government coverage. Be sure to check all this with a lawyer or estate planner, as
laws can vary from state to state.

---

*"Should my parents buy long term care insurance
to help pay for their nursing home care?"*

A huge market for long term care insurance has developed, and
starting in 1997, premiums for certain policies qualify as a tax
deduction if these costs plus other medical expenses exceed 7.5
percent of adjusted gross income. First, figure out if your parents
can afford the premiums—they should never exceed 5 percent of
their income. If their assets are less than the cost of one year in a
nursing home, this kind of insurance probably is not a sound investment. If you decide to buy a policy, (they are often a very good
investment) be sure you or someone you trust reads the fine print
and asks the following:

— Does the policy cover both home care and nursing home
   care?

— How much is the daily benefit?

— How long will the benefits last?

— What is the deductible/elimination period?

— Does the policy have a maximum lifetime benefit?

— Do the premiums increase, or are they fixed?

— Does the policy contain a premium-waiver option, allowing

— one to stop paying premiums when collecting benefits?

— Does the policy provide for reduced benefits if the policy

— lapses after a specific number of years?

— Does the plan offer an inflation-protection option to cover

— escalating costs of care?

— Do late payers have a grace period?

— Are there age limits or specific pre-existing health conditions?

— Can the policy be upgraded to provide higher benefits for a

— longer time period?

— Are there exclusions for certain illnesses?

And most important, the older you are the more expensive your premiums will be, so start thinking about how to pay for your falling-apart years before you fall apart.

"Now that my parents are needing caregivers in their home, what's the best way to find the right person?"

Here's where you should do some sleuthing. Best way is word-of-mouth from a reliable source who's actually retained someone for more than six months. Ask around; try ministers, teachers, call home health care agencies, companion services, and of course, ask your parents' physician for referrals. Be wary of anybody who won't give you a list of people he/she has taken care of, and when you get

the list, check them out carefully. Telephone them, or their families, and ask specific questions such as, "How long did Fifi work for your mother, and what exactly were her responsibilities each day?" We recommend, if possible, that you or another family member drive by the prospective caregiver's house or apartment just to see that it checks out. We've heard about people who give non-existing addresses, hoping to get live-in positions.

Offer a trial period when you do hire somebody. Clarify in your mind exactly what you expect of this caregiver, and write a brief job description. You can read it and check prospective employees qualifications on the telephone. We've queried many caregivers to determine what their concerns are, and their list goes something like this: don't be argumentative, pay me on time, don't be suspicious that I'm ripping you off, give me reasonable time off, be considerate of my feelings, and make sure the check doesn't bounce. Be sure you have a contract, spell out the hours you expect someone to work, provide workers compensation, pay for overtime, be specific with responsibilities, and discuss personal habits such as smoking, and apparel (uniforms?). If the caregiver will be accompanying your parent into a dining room at a retirement community, read the rules, as some facilities don't permit caregivers in dining areas. Just about everybody wants to avoid problems with the Immigration Department, so make sure there are no unpleasant surprises here. If you expect Miss Priss to have access to your parents accounts make sure that safeguards are in place. It's wise to remove checkbooks and valuables. You may go through three or four people before you find the right fit for Mom and Dad, but keep trying, there are some fabulous people out there for whom caregiving is second nature. We have a believe-it-or-not story which is outrageous, but true. Mrs. Iceland was taken to the Chevrolet dealership one day by her caregiver. The caregiver told her she wanted a car. She picked it out, and had Mrs. Iceland sign with an X on the dotted line (because Mrs. Iceland couldn't write) and left the dealership. When Mr. Iceland found out he was furious and of course took the car back and fired the caregiver. These things happen and right under your own nose too!

In moving clients into retirement communities, we met a new group dubbed "the resistors." One way or another, these Seniors will find a way to sabotage the move or postpone it to a point that moving no longer becomes an alternative. In reading the list of types of resistors see which ones sound familiar:

▌ Losing important documents which are essential to the move.

▌ Forgetting or canceling appointments.

▌ Not answering the door when you have scheduled an appointment.

▌ Being rude.

▌ Procrastinating.

- Making excuses.

- Feigning ineptitude when competence is apparent.

- Breaking promises.

- Breaking deadlines.

- Aggressive, insubordinate behavior causing discomfort for family and caregivers.

If you, the person helping the Senior, can remove yourself emotionally, it may be easier to understand and work with those who are moving. In essence, the resistance encountered most likely springs from fear. Try to determine the real issues and address them. Don't allow yourself to be sucked into a situation where your ego and pride infringe on the Senior's dignity.

20.

"We Decided to Move When My Wife Closed the Kitchen," and Other Gems From Seniors and Their Children

W<!-- -->e have spent many hours listening to Seniors, asking them questions while doing research for this book. There were plenty of times when we just had to sit back and hear them out. They told us they were tired of other people telling them what was on their minds. Following is a sampling of what they had to say.

The majority of retirement community residents made the decision to move themselves, and most had help from family members. Family members proved to be the largest source of information about retirement communities, but it was an eye-opener to us to learn the number of people who didn't even visit a community before they moved. But when we asked if they understood the differences in the types of communities, a large percentage assured us they did. Who stays in all those overly decorated guest rooms? Certainly not potential residents. Statistics tell us most Seniors don't spend the night in their new retirement community before moving in. We asked why the Seniors moved, and compiled these responses:

- I felt lonely and isolated.

- Medical services would be available.

- No more responsibility for maintaining the house.

- To be near family and friends.

- Wanted a secure, safe atmosphere.

- Important to have a warm, friendly attitude of staff and residents.

- Needed to have a good overall feeling of community.

- I was tired of doing everything for myself.

- Weather and location.

- Wanted to travel and not worry about their home.

- Wanted to meet new people.

- Wanted more recreational and social activities.

- My family thought it was time for me to move.

- Didn't want to be a burden to my family.

- I could no longer drive.

- I could no longer do things for myself.

- I didn't want to move, my kids made the decision for me.

As we listened, we jotted down what we heard, and we asked them to comment on anything they felt—we wanted them to be open and honest and not feel intimidated by others. Here's what was on their minds:

- "I just didn't want to own anything any more."

■ "I liked the incentive program they had at Forest Glen."

■ "It makes me depressed to see people in wheelchairs."

■ "I didn't want someone else to make the choice for me."

■ "It took longer for me to feel comfortable and to adjust to my new surroundings than I thought."

■ "My wife and I never agreed on anything and we sure didn't agree on this move."

■ "I didn't want my children to *put* me in a retirement home."

■ "Don't forget we ate all those preservatives so we're all living longer."

■ "The staff is like a second family to me."

■ "It's just like being on a cruise; they do everything for you."

■ "If you think you should move and don't want to move now, when do you think the right time will be?"

■ "We moved because it's easier to go to a community with your spouse."

■ "Your peers are older and won't be around as long as your family."

■ "I was tired of eating with a book beside my plate."

■ "I was watching the clock and said we had to do something before we get decrepit."

- "You have to give up some things to gain others."

- "I never did drive and Harold couldn't drive any more, so there we were stuck."

- "Best thing we ever did."

- "My health wasn't going to get any better."

- "All our old neighbors died and the neighborhood started going to pot."

- "My kids fought the idea of me coming to a community. They thought it was an old folks home."

- "My son said, 'I feel so lucky to have parents who have made up their own minds and I can see them living happily.'"

- "Never do today what you can put off till tomorrow."

- "Make up your mind before somebody else does it for you."

- "My wife closed the kitchen 10 years ago."

- "We felt overwhelmed selling our house and dividing up our belongings."

- "I don't want to live with my kids and I don't want them living with me."

- "You can't replace friends, you just make new ones."

- "You have pretty much a worry-free life."

- "Don't get old."

- "I don't want to live any place where I can't have a pop in my own room."

- "I think I meet a lot of new people here, but I can't remember who they are when I see them around."

We wondered why some people hadn't moved, and where they were currently living. Most lived in their own homes and had been there for over 15 years. A larger number had never inquired about retirement communities, but the information they did receive came from family members. A lot of these folks were negative about retirement communities, largely because they had never visited another person living in one, and didn't understand that there were differing types. The prevalent attitude seemed to be that these were "old folks homes." Oddly enough, when we inquired if they would consider moving to a retirement community most said "yes." When we asked what they thought was perhaps the best time to consider moving, one clever woman told us, "When my children stop moving back home."

Here is what was on the minds of those Seniors that wanted to stay where they were. Do these ring a bell?

- "I like where I am."

- "I'm not ready to move."

- "I'm still able to care for myself."

- "Maybe I'll move when I get older and don't care."

- "My family lives with me now."

- "I don't like to see all old people, they're depressing."

- "My condo location is good."

- "I don't want to lose my independence."

- "I want to have control over my life."

- "How would you like someone to tell you what time to eat dinner."

- "I like to bake at Christmas and there aren't ovens in some of those retirement communities."

- "I think my children should take care of me in my second childhood since I took care of them in their first."

- "I think retirement communities are great, but I don't have any idea when I should start looking."

- "I know a lot of folks who are alone, but they don't want to say they're lonely."

- "It feels kind of unnatural to think about moving out of my family home."

∎ "I used to love to cook and entertain, but not many of our friends want to go out at night, so now we eat TV dinners most of the time."

∎ "Staying active and keeping involved are key ingredients to remaining in your own home."

As we talked to the children of these Seniors, we saw things from a different perspective. Here are a few of the kids' thoughts:

∎ "It's really difficult when you have to make the decisions for your parents such as where they're going to live."

∎ "I read brochures from four different retirement communities and was more confused than ever."

∎ "My parents were just not able to organize the move themselves. Fortunately, we lived close enough to help them."

∎ "My Dad wanted me to do the legwork in finding the places and that meant I had to go twice to each community—once for the research and then I had to take him back. It was just too much."

∎ "I started resenting the time it took going all over looking at places and then decided to hire a person who had been to hundreds and could assess our situation. She was fantastic, suggested the perfect spot, and the fee was reasonable."

- "We all decided it was important for the community to have a homelike feeling."

- "You must have to have a Ph.D. in retirement communities to discover what's different about each one."

- "I couldn't stand to see Mom so lonely after Dad died."

- "After Dad moved, I didn't feel so guilty at not seeing him a lot because he was around people and had plenty of activities."

- "My mother resisted moving and is still annoyed that she's there."

- "My Dad needs a lot of emotional support and we wanted a place with a strong staff."

- "I got sick of running over to fix her house when mine was deteriorating."

- "We're spending our money on our parents when maybe we should have gotten them long term care insurance, but we didn't know enough about it."

- "We never realized how much we'd have to pay to get the kind of care we wanted for our parents."

- "We found that talking to the residents was a good way to find out if this was a good place for Mom.

- "People should ask what percentage of the residents have

some form of dementia because the management doesn't want to talk about it; you might not want to put your parent there."

■ "How come they don't have doctors who come to the community?"

■ "I didn't want my parents to move because I didn't want them in an old folks home. Boy was I pleasantly surprised to see what some of them are really like!"

■ "One of the best things to come out of the move was for Aunt Gladys and her family to take a good look at her financial picture."

■ "Well, my sister and I hadn't been very close but when we had to coordinate getting our parents into a different living situation, we started to like each other more."

■ "It made all the difference in Dad's attitude to find a place where he could take Cootie, his old hunting dog."

We were surprised at some of our findings. For instance, 95% of the people who moved to retirement communities said that they were glad they had. Something that really amazed us was the attitude of many residents toward their peers with disabilities and impairments. People who move into a retirement community and later become disabled already have the friendship and support of their peers. But for the new resident who is limited physically, it's not so easy—people look down on those less fortunate.

It was quite apparent that the children had far more influence on their parents' decisions in lower income communities than in higher socio-economic brackets. Isn't it interesting that the response to the question, "I enjoy maintaining my home?" was largely "no," and yet, these people didn't want to move...why? Fear, denial, and lack of communication are often the biggest obstacles to making the proper decision. When the subject is openly discussed all the unspoken concerns can be addressed. One Senior organized a weekend specifically to talk about what had always been an uncomfortable topic. He told us, "I felt so great after we spent the weekend with our son and we were able to open up, laughing and crying and just saying what was on our minds, and I could tell he felt better, too." Oftentimes, finding an answer is just as simple as asking a question.

Glossary

ACCESSORY APARTMENT—a completely separate living unit inside a single-family home. A popular housing option for Seniors who want to stay in their homes, and a potential source of caregiving between an older person and neighbor, providing the convenience of physical closeness while maintaining privacy. Provides additional income to landlord, and low rent for tenant.

ACTIVITIES OF DAILY LIVING—a term used to denote areas of assistance. Some ADL's are: bathing, dressing, feeding, transferring into or out of chair or bed, continence, and toileting.

ADMINISTRATION ON AGING—Office of Human Development Services, HUD—principal federal agency responsible for administering most provisions of Older Americans Act. Works with state and local agencies, concentrates on interests of elderly.

ADULT DAY CARE CENTER—a place that provides activities and meals for Seniors plus interaction with peers and resources.

ADULT FOSTER HOME—Licensed family-oriented homes that take in older people who pay for room and board. Usually fewer than four Seniors live in one home.

ASSISTED LIVING FACILITY—a residential facility not licensed as a nursing home that provides personal care and support services to elderly who need help with daily activities. These communities go by a variety of names and are often affiliated with independent living communities or nursing care facilities.

ASSISTED HOUSING—also called **SUBSIDIZED HOUSING**—Lodging that receives financial assistance through a federal, state, local, non-profit or for profit program. Assistance can be through rent subsidy, interest subsidy or contributions toward capital cost. Subsidized or assisted housing usually has a public benefit, such as for low or moderate income or special-interest individuals.

BOARD AND CARE HOME—also known as **DOMICILIARY CARE, PERSONAL CARE, RESIDENTIAL CARE**—living arrangement, usually a house in a residential neighborhood of private or shared sleeping rooms and bathrooms, with meals and housekeeping included. Some homes provide supervision, personal care services, transportation and outings, and others offer nothing other than a bed. Board and care homes cater to people with varying disabilities including Alzheimer's and related dementia patients, physically disabled and those who are just old with nowhere else to go.

CAREGIVER—someone who takes care of another person.

ATTORNEY-IN-FACT—an individual empowered to act on behalf of another according to terms of a power of attorney or durable power of attorney.

COGNITIVE IMPAIRMENT—one of those words in an insurance policy or contract that means you've lost it and you can't take care of yourself without supervision, as with Alzheimer's.

COMMUNITY SPOUSE—a Medicaid term for the spouse not confined to a nursing home and not applying for Medicaid.

CONGREGATE LIVING CENTER, also known as **RESIDENCE HOTEL** or **RESIDENCE FOR SENIORS**—an apartment-like facility in which Seniors capable of independent living have their own apartment and may receive, sometimes for an extra fee, hotel-like services and amenities. Many of these complexes were built with government subsidies.

CONDOMINIUM—one's dwelling and generally the land it's on, with shared ownership of common areas. Each unit or dwelling can be financed separately.

CONGREGATE HOUSING—a catch-all term to describe living arrangements for those who need or want to live close to others for mutual support or assistance. This generic term includes facilities having a private space for each resident in addition to shared common areas and services. A college dorm is congregate housing, as is a group home for mentally retarded adolescents, and an assisted living facility for Seniors.

CONTINUING CARE RETIREMENT COMMUNITY—a housing option which promises to provide one or more elements of care for the duration of resident's life for additional medical services provided. Provisions to subsidize residents who become unable to pay their monthly fee is provided.

CONSERVATORSHIP—the result of a court proceeding which declares an individual unable to take care of decision-making and legal matters. The court will appoint another individual to make the decisions, and he or she is known as a **CONSERVATOR**. A similar term is **GUARDIAN**..

COOPERATIVE HOUSING—residents are stockholders in a corporation which owns the building in which they live. Residents have occupancy rights for their individual units, rather than owning the unit. Prospective buyers must be approved by a board prior to closing.

CUSTODIAL CARE—a level of care required by a person unable to perform the activities of daily living alone that doesn't require professional services such as a therapist. It's what most people receive by attendants in nursing facilities and Assisted Living.

DURABLE POWER OF ATTORNEY—a document permitting an individual to designate a third person to act in his or her behalf. This is a useful device for management of one's personal and financial affairs in the event of mental or physical incapacity. The person setting it up can include instructions, guidelines, or limitations as he wishes.

ECHO (Elder Cottage Housing Opportunity)—a complete, small house temporarily on the same lot as a single family dwelling. This encourages informal support enabling an older person or couple to remain close to others, yet retain some independence.

ESTATE TAX—levied on the things you own or valuables on any amount exceeding $600,000. A spouse can leave any amount to one another without it being taxed, but on the death of the surviving spouse an estate tax could pop up.

GERIATRIC CARE MANAGEMENT—programs to facilitate and coordinate services to the elderly, such as referring them to legal and housing services.

HEALTH CARE FINANCING ADMINISTRATION—a branch of the U.S. Department of Health and Human Services concerned with the financing and delivery of health care to aged, disabled and poor.

HEALTH CARE PROXY—a document permitted in some states allowing one person to designate another to make health care decisions in the event he or she becomes incapacitated, also called a

DURABLE POWER OF ATTORNEY FOR HEALTH CAREHEALTH MAINTENANCE ORGANIZATION (HMO)—an organization whose members can receive medical services from participating providers (physicians and clinics) for a periodic flat fee. HMOs typically have no or very low deductible and co-payment provisions.

HOME EQUITY CONVERSION—the process of borrowing against the equity one has built up in a home.

HOME SHARING/HOUSE MATCHING—a kind of shared housing arrangement in which two non-related people are matched with the intention of living together, sharing expenses and allowing for mutual support and assistance. Sleeping quarters are generally private, with the rest of the home area shared.

HOMES FOR THE AGED—a generic term for residential facilities for older people who need or want some kind of help or support with activities of daily living. In many cities' yellow pages, a wide variety of Senior housing is listed under this cheerful sounding title.

INTERMEDIATE CARE FACILITY (ICF)—a type of nursing home providing care less extensive than that of a skilled nursing facility. Patients in an ICF may need the care of a registered nurse only occasionally, not on a 24-hour basis.

IN-HOME SERVICES or **IN-HOME FOSTER CARE**—refers to home health aid, family respite services, visiting and telephone reassurance, driving to appointments, and minor home maintenance. These services are designed to enable Seniors to stay in their homes as long as possible.

JOINT TENANCY—a form of co-ownership between two or more people who own an item of real or personal property. At the death of each joint tenant, the deceased's interest passes automatically to the survivor. Also called **JOINT TENANCY WITH RIGHTS OF SURVIVORSHIP**.

LIFECARE RETIREMENT COMMUNITY—a kind of continuing care living arrangement which promises to provide all levels of care, including acute care and physicians' services, for the duration of life in exchange for the payment of an entrance fee. Care is provided in a facility under ownership and supervision of the provider on or adjacent to the premises. It is a "pay-as-you-go" system, and by contrast to Continuing Care, provides needed services but usually with additional fees.

LOCAL HOUSING AUTHORITY—the government's agency responsible for administering public housing subsidies at the local level.

LIVING WILL—a document that allows you to spell out your medical treatment wishes (usually about life support) if you are unable to speak for yourself. Witnessing requirements vary from state to state and should be followed to the letter. It is part of an Advance Directive for Health Care and differs from a Health Care Power of Attorney in that a living will doesn't appoint an agent and, in many states, applies only to terminal illness or persistent vegetative state. Because the living will applies only in narrowly and sometimes unclearly defined circumstances, it's best to have both a living will and Health Care Power of Attorney or to combine them both in one Advance Directive.

LONG TERM CARE— any type of support and care a person may need over an extended period of time. It includes assistance with bathing and dressing, meal preparation, shopping, housecleaning, transportation, shopping, or a stay in a facility up to a skilled nursing facility.

LONG TERM CARE INSURANCE—a specific insurance written to help cover costs of long term care within a nursing facility, other types of settings and a variety of home health care situations.

MEDICAID—a welfare program jointly administered by the federal and state governments to provide health care to aged, blind, disabled and families with dependent children who are poor. Medicaid will provide benefits for eligible individuals who require long term custodial care. Benefits vary among states.

MEDICARE—the principal health care program of the federal government, which is supposed to provide health care insurance for those over 65. Part A is hospital insurance and Part B, supplementary insurance, is optional, meaning you pay. It provides additional coverage to pay for physician's services. We all know the system's due for an overhaul, and although providing extensive benefits for hospital outpatient and physician care, Medicare in its current state pays for very few benefits for the elderly requiring long term custodial care.

MEDIGAP INSURANCE—the buzzword for health insurance policies designed to cover the deductible, co-payments and other gaps that exist under Medicare. These Medigap policies don't pay benefits for long term care. These policies are also called **MEDICARE SUPPLEMENTAL POLICIES**.

MULTIPLE SUPPORT AGREEMENT—comes under the tax laws and allows several family members to take turns claiming an elderly parent or other relative as a dependent. If the criteria are met, the people in the agreement alternate claiming the personal exemption and medical expense deductions of the dependent relative.

REFUND SYSTEM IN CCRC or **LIFECARE COMMUNITY WITHOUT EQUITY**—the means whereby the buyer puts down more than the actual cost of the unit. In the event he doesn't move in, the buyer then gets back a percentage of the cost of the unit.

RESIDENTIAL CARE FACILITY—a housing option for frail Seniors who need custodial care or assistance with activities of daily living. Most of the care can be provided by licensed practical nurses, CNAs and other people who aren't highly trained.

RETIREMENT COMMUNITY—a broad catch-all term referring to a type of housing (can be high rise, individual houses or trailers, you name it) usually designed for and marketed to older people. Units can be purchased or rented, and there are often recreational and social activities on the premises. Supportive services are offered in some, and retirement communities run the gamut from a plushy country-club design for active healthy retirees to independent Alzheimer's facilities.

REVERSE MORTGAGE—a form of loan arrangement under which an elderly home owner may access the equity in his home. With the home pledged as security, there may be a line of credit against the home that the owner taps by writing a check, or a second option is for the Senior to receive a regular amount from the lender, with each check increasing the amount of the debt against the house.

REVOCABLE LIVING TRUST—a legal instrument established during the life of the grantor which permits him to change any or all of the terms at any time. A living trust is also known as an **INTER VIVOS** trust. Many older people set up revocable living trusts so that there is someone to manage their financial affairs if they become unable to do so.

SKILLED NURSING FACILITY (SNF)—can stand alone or be part of another facility providing the highest level of nursing home care. Registered nurses provide round-the-clock care, and Medicare pays some benefits for the elderly in a SNF.

SSI (Supplemental Security Income)—a government cash handout program designed to help low income old, blind and disabled.

Comparative Cost Worksheet

	Parents Monthly Home Costs	Monthly Costs at the Chatfield
Rent / Mortgage	_____	_____
Medical costs	_____	_____
Property insurance	_____	_____
Property taxes	_____	_____
Utilities	_____	_____
Home maintenance	_____	_____
Security systems	_____	_____
Gardening	_____	_____
Housecleaning	_____	_____
Food	_____	_____
Entertainment	_____	_____
Household supplies	_____	_____
Transportation	_____	_____
Car payments, up- keep, insurance	_____	_____

Visitor's Checklist

Name: _____

Address: _____

Telephone: _____

Contact: Title: _____

Date Visited: _____

Age of Facility: _____ Overall rating: _____

Structural rating: _____ Service rating: _____

TYPE OF FACILITY

Planned Adult Community: _____

Independent Retirement Living: _____

Residential Facility for Elderly (assisted care): _____

Continuing Care: _____

Life-Care: _____

Skilled Nursing: _____

Alzheimers: _____

Management Group: _____

Religious Affiliation: _____

APPROXIMATE COSTS

Entry fee or deposit: _____ Refundable: _____

Buy-in: _____ Monthly assessment: _____

Monthly rental fee: _____

RESIDENTIAL DEMOGRAPHICS

Number of apartments: _____ Number of residents: _____

Ratio of women to men: _____ Average age: _____

WAITING LIST

Yes: ____ No: ____ Length of Wait: _____ What accommodation: _____

MISCELLANEOUS

SSI Participant: _____ Subsidized: _____

Accredited (state): _____

Long term care insurance offered: _____

	Yes	No	Comments
General Atmosphere & Condition			
Exterior Appearance			
Appealing			
Landscaping well done			
Attractive entrance / driveway			
Neighborhood			
Construction Details			
High-rise			
1–4 stories			
Cluster units			
Cottages			
Elevators			
Interior Appearance			
Entrance Hall inviting			
Fresh flowers in entry area			
Light and airy			
Warm feeling			
Well decorated			
Home-like atmosphere			
Hotel-like atmosphere			
Clean and odor-free			
Uncluttered			
Furniture clean & in good repair			
Location			
Warm			
Temperate			
Natural setting			
Near ocean			
In suburbs			
In country			
Downtown			
Traffic noise			
Has a view			
Lots of trees			

	Yes	No	Comments
Access Features			
Near public transportation			
Near churches			
Close to shopping centers			
Close to hospitals			
Outdoor Features			
Areas for sitting			
Covered walkways			
Walking path on property			
Transportation			
Provided for medical needs			
Provided for personal needs			
Scheduled			
Unscheduled			
Limo available			
Parking			
Secure parking provided			
Indoor parking			
Staff & Residents			
Staff Behavior			
Interested & warm reaction to my visit			
Residents treated with care & respect			
Residents' Behavior			
Residents seem in good spirits			
Appropriate dress (no robes)			
Dining and Diet			
Dining Room			
Attractive dining room			
Fireplace in dining room			
Dress code at dinner			
Number of Meals Offered Daily			
1 meal plan			
2 meal plan			

	Yes	No	Comments
Meals Offered Daily (cont'd.)			
3 meal plan			
3 meals served daily			
Assigned Seating			
1 meal			
All meals			
No meals			
Service Style			
Cafeteria			
Restaurant			
Tray service available if needed			
All-tray service			
Buffets			
Breakfast			
Lunch			
Dinner			
Dining Choices			
Flexible dining hours			
Meals served at fixed time only			
Meals appetizing & tasteful			
Meals sufficient quantity			
Breakfast-Lunch-Dinner			
Fixed menu			
Choice of foods			
Salad bar			
Big meal in the middle of the day			
Other Food Choices			
Substitutes available			
Fresh fruits & vegetables			
Snacks available between meals			
Dietary & religious needs considered			
Ice cream parlor			

	Yes	No	Comments
Liquor			
Bar			
In own room			
No liquor in facility			
Wine cellar			
Wine served with dinner			
Dining Features			
Fresh flowers on tables			
Private dining available			
Guest meals available			
Walkers allowed in dining area			
Wheelchairs allowed in dining area			
Separate assisted-care dining			
Main kitchen accessible to residents			
Activities			
Fitness Activities			
Exercise Director			
Floor exercise classes			
Pool exercise classes			
Personal Trainer			
Croquet			
Golf course			
Gymnasium equipment (some)			
Horseshoe pits			
Lawn bowling green			
Outdoor activity area			
Par course			
Pool table			
Putting green			
Shuffleboard court			
Stables for horseback riding			
Jacuzzi			
Massage			

	Yes	No	Comments
Fitness Activities (cont'd.)			
Sauna			
Steam pool			
Swimming pool			
Tennis			
Whirlpool bath			
Bicycling			
Hiking nearby			
Walking nearby			
Communication Equipment & Media			
Fax available			
In-house newspaper			
In-house T.V. station			
Activity Areas Available			
Conference rooms			
Flower workshop			
Game room (separate)			
Library			
Recreation room			
Sewing room			
Shop area			
Television in common rooms			
Theater			
VCR available to residents			
Computer room			
Chapel			
Presentations & Planned Activities			
Program Director			
Arts and crafts			
Educational			
Cocktail parties			
Dances			
Excursions			

	Yes	No	Comments
Movies			
Music before or after dinner			
Musical presentations			
Speakers			
Special occasion parties			
Gardening			
Residents involved in charitable projects			
Accommodations			
Maintenance and Repairs			
Provided			
At extra costs			
Individual decorating permitted			
Accommodation Features			
Buy-in (no ownership)			
Own			
Rent			
Living quarters close to main activities			
Individual temperature controls			
Air-conditioning			
Fireplace in rooms			
Studio, no kitchen			
Studio with kitchen			
Alcove studio			
Common bath area			
Room without kitchen			
1 bedroom, sink or toilet only			
1 bedroom, 1 bath			
1 bedroom plus sitting room, 2 baths			
2 bedroom, 1 bath			
2 bedroom plus sitting room, 2 baths			
Penthouse			
Furnished			

	Yes	No	Comments
Accommodation Features (cont'd.)			
Unfurnished			
Shared rooms			
Common Living Area Features			
Main living room			
Common living areas on each floor			
Fireplaces			
Solarium			
Television			
Cable available			
Cable at extra charge			
Storage			
Adequate closets			
Extra outside storage available			
Deck or Patio			
Private			
Enclose on ground floor			
Kitchen Features			
Kitchen on each floor			
All rooms, no kitchens			
Kitchenette			
Full kitchen in apartment			
Kitchenette with burners; no oven / oven			
Cleaning			
Linens provided			
Linens provided for a fee			
Linens changed for residents			
Personal laundry service (how often)			
Laundry rooms available to residents			
Housekeeping service			
Weekly			

	Yes	No	Comments
Bi-Monthly			
Monthly			
Bath Features			
Tub & shower combination			
Tub only			
Shower only			
Safety / Security Features			
Grab bars			
Electronic security system			
Emergency call system			
In bath			
In living room			
Firewall staircase construction			
Indoor sprinklers			
Intercom system			
Safety check for residents			
Security officers			
Accessible to persons with limited ability			
Wide halls			
Medical			
Medical Services			
Infirmary or medical office			
Prearranged access to skilled nursing facility			
Counseling for psychiatric therapy			
Personal Care			
Assisted care			
In own unit			
Physicians			
Own required			
Available on daily basis			
Available on weekly basis			
On-call 24-hours			
No physicians			

	Yes	No	Comments
Nurses			
LVN available on daily basis			
LVN available on weekly basis			
RN available on daily basis			
RN available on weekly basis			
No nurses			
Staff			
24-hour on-site medical staff			
Medically trained staff			
First aid & CPR training for staff			
Information for Prospective Residents			
Good staff reception			
Video of facility			
Brochures helpful and well-done			
Complimentary lunch			
Complimentary dinner			
Miscellaneous Features and Options			
24-hour on-site management			
Receptionist			
Reciprocal use of facilities			
Pets allowed			
Resident Participation			
Resident Council			
Resident participation in management			
Non-Resident Options			
Guest room accommodations			
Free apartment available on trial basis			
Religious Needs			
Chapel			
Chaplain			
Religious services held at facility			

	Yes	No	Comments
Smoking Provisions			
Smoking in personal rooms			
Smoking room			
No Smoking anywhere in facility			

Index

A

Activities of Daily Living (ADLs) 125, 227
Adult Family Homes 65
Adult Foster Care 65, 227
Alzheimer's 30, 35, 111, 116, 139–46
Alzheimer's Association 38
American Association of Retired Persons (AARP) 16, 22, 31, 155
American Healthcare Association 137–38
apartments (*see* Senior apartments)
Arthritis 70
assisted living 93, 111, 119, 125–28, 227

B

balance problems 71
boarding and care 66, 68, 143, 154–61, 228

C

Certified Financial Planners 29, 205
Charitable Remainder Trust 121
condominiums 59, 229
conservatorships 204, 229
continuing care 19, 33, 34, 105–11, 114, 229
contractors 188–91
convalescent hospital 130
cooperatives 59
custodial care 154, 230

D

downsizing 102
Durable Power of Attorney 230

E

ECHO housing 61–62
Elder Law 205
Elder Law Attorney 29, 205
Eldercare Locator 31, 61
estate tax 230

F

family care homes 155
finances 40–42, 147
fire codes 89

G

Ground Fault Interrupters (GFIs) 73, 75
Granny Flats (see ECHO housing)

H

health issues 44–45
Health Care Financing Administration 133, 230
Health Care Proxy 230
hearing loss 70
home-matching programs 61, 231
housing options 58–68
HMOs 231
HUD 148–51, 227

I

Independent Retirement Community 36, 86–94

L

Lifecare 23, 33, 34, 105–111, 188, 232
living will 153, 232

Long Term Care Accreditation
  Program 137
ong term care insurance 116, 117,
  122, 208, 212, 233
Long Term Care Ombudsman 130,
  150

M

meals 103, 112
Meals on Wheels 80, 150
Medicaid 30, 133, 211, 233
Medicare 80, 97, 103, 106, 111, 129–
  133
Medigap insurance 233
mobile homes 58
moving checklist 173
moving companies 163
moving insurance 166
multigenerational housing 149

N

National Association of Professional
  Geriatric Managers 214
National Council on Aging 192
non-use assessment 19

P

pets 91, 101

Planned Adult Community 81

R

Realtors 180–88
Refund System in CCRC 234
rental community 95–104
retirement hotel 65
reverse mortgage 121, 234
Revocable Living Trust 234

S

Seniors apartment house 60, 66,
  227, 228
shared housing 64–65, 231
skilled nursing facility 97, 103, 116,
  129–138, 235
SSI 148–81
subsidized housing 147–50
supplemental insurance 30, 193

V

vision loss 70

W

wheelchairs and walkers 98–99

Y

You Are Not Alone (YANA) 79

About the Authors

Donna Quinn Robbins is the founder and owner of Ultimate Moves, a company serving Seniors in transition. Ultimate Moves was started when Donna recognized the need of many Seniors for clear and concise guidance on the complex issues older adults face as they explore their lifestyle options. Donna feels that by educating our aging population and their families on the many communities and options available, Seniors can plan their move and ease the burden accompanying the change. Armed with her eight-page checklist, Donna visited hundreds of retirement communities to gather complete data, all of which she has used to help families decide upon the most appropriate living situation. In addition to being a consultant, she works with many retirement communities as a space planner, move-in coordinator, and designer. Donna has years of experience in public speaking through seminars, focus groups, and lectures. Her column, "Seniors Ask" appeared in a Bay Area newspaper, and she has appeared on news programs answering questions of interest to children of Seniors. She also volunteers at Senior Centers and has served on the Committee for Senior Olympics.

Sarah Morse is an editor and writer. For part of the research for *Moving Mom and Dad,* she visited many retirement communities, and currently volunteers in one. As an editor and writer of travel books and articles, her work has appeared in numerous journals and periodicals, including *The New York Times, The Asian Wall Street Journal,* the *Cornell Quarterly, Island Scene,* and the *Guide to Retirement Living.* She is a member of the American Society on Aging.